The Sacred Place of Exile

The Sacred Place of Exile

Pioneering Women and the Need for a New
Women's Missionary Movement

Carla Brewington

WIPF & STOCK · Eugene, Oregon

THE SACRED PLACE OF EXILE
Pioneering Women and the Need for a New Women's Missionary Movement

Wipf & Stock
An Imprint of Wipf and Stock Publishers
199 W. 8th Ave., Suite 3
Eugene, OR 97401
www.wipfandstock.com

ISBN 13: 978-1-62032-284-0
Manufactured in the U.S.A.

To the women both past and present,
who have risked all,
so that the gospel may be preached to the ends of the earth.
From the high places of Tibet to the jungles of Burma,
to the borderlands of Israel,
women are bringing the mercy and love of God
to war zones, limited-access countries, and disaster areas.
This book is dedicated to you.

You will leave everything you love most:

this is the arrow that the bow of exile shoots first.

You will know how salty another's bread tastes and how hard it is

to ascend and descend another's stairs . . .

DANTE

Contents

Foreword

THIS BOOK IS ABOUT women wild for God and for things of God: whatever the cost. They arrive at this passion out of exile, living at the margins, knowing the reality of rejection and pain. Precisely out of that reality, comes their unique and urgent importance as witnesses to the reality of God's Kingdom.

Carla Brewington not only writes about these women, she is one of them. From the first day we met until now, she has always struck me this way. She stands in the world at an angle oblique to much that passes as ordinary or typical. Carla is not your "run of the mill" anything. She is a particular person with her own particular history, relationships, and passions.

Carla's vision and voice sound clearly in this book. Plainspoken, direct, intense, bold: these are certainly words that capture some of who Carla is, and how Carla lives. Her personal and spiritual journey has amplified these qualities. Carla's political and communitarian instincts are those of a person who feels life at the margins, whose empathy with suffering people flows with ready identification and support, whose distinctiveness makes community both difficult and essential. Her own experiences of pain and struggle, of rejection and exclusion mean she comes with credibility to the topic and the vocation she writes about here.

What I find most moving in Carla, however, is that in the midst of her struggling story is the presence of illuminating joy. When we first met, Carla had yet to live into the embrace of God's radical love in Jesus Christ. Anger, disappointment, struggle, and disillusionment understandably pervaded her story. Carla was thrashing her way towards God. The outcome of that was by no means clear when she suddenly vanished. As though in mid-sentence, she left Berkeley and took her dramatic story with her, suspended for me for almost twenty-five years. When we met again three years ago, I was stunned by God's intervening joy in Carla's life. The illuminating light Carla bore did not and does not mask her journey or the suffering world with which she identifies. Rather, the light of God's truth and grace in Carla's own exilic story shines in the midst of what is raw and unfinished, transformed and being transformed.

The authenticity, conviction, and urgency of this book arise from Carla's own story. As she shares her fascinating scholarship about radical women over the past centuries, she speaks with her own God-shaped vision, and testifies to the God who has radically spoken in Jesus Christ—to the world, to other women, and to her. That Word comes with transformative, life-giving power that gathers in and binds up the brokenhearted, that never steps away from those at the margins, and that confronts, reorders, and restores all other power. This is the God who knows and loves the radicalized women Carla has in mind here, who shares their pain, who strengthens them in their giftedness and in their exile, and who demonstrates through them aspects of God's attentive care that only they could offer. This book is a call to women at the margins to form communal lives that embody together their response to the radical, costly love of Jesus Christ for people in pain.

The core of Carla's life and of the women God will gather is this: a whole-life devotion to Jesus Christ. One that is radical and necessary, wild and demanding, needed and difficult, personal and public, awkward and costly, disruptive and hopeful.

For the sake of Kingdom love, Carla Brewington is saying to women, "O taste and see that the Lord is good." It will take your whole life. It's radical and good!

Mark Labberton
Lloyd John Ogilvie Associate Professor of Preaching
Director, Lloyd John Ogilvie Institute of Preaching
Fuller Theological Seminary, Pasadena, California USA

Preface

MANY YEARS AGO I had a vision of forming what I then called a "monastic-missionary" community. I thought people would scoff at the idea but I drew up plans, made lists, and ached for a community of likeminded women who would come together to do their part for the kingdom of God. After a while I packed away the hopes and dreams for that vision and placed it high on a shelf where it gathered much dust over the years. Now, I believe, is the time to bring that vision back out again; this time with a few revisions. Instead of a monastic-missionary community, I envision many monastic-missionary/friaristic communities which are part of a new women's missionary movement.

Much of the missionary world is still not listening to the voices of women who have been denied access to ministry. My task here is not to make an argument for more women in top leadership positions within existing missionary organizations, but to present a case for a new way of seeing, a deeper way of understanding, a fresh hermeneutic. This new hermeneutic will build a bridge from the missionary community to the rich reservoir of outsider women ready to take their place to meet the task ahead.

This new way of seeing is actually an old way of understanding what it meant to follow Jesus. There were women disciples who banded together and followed him. They were from various backgrounds and of different ages, but their goal was the same—to be as close to Jesus as possible and to go wherever he went, no matter what the cost. Because of the scope of this book, I will not go into the scriptural account of these women, but only to say that they include the likes of Mary Magdalene and other women whom Jesus loved deeply. They stayed with him until the end and waited at the tomb as well. And it was a woman who first ran to tell the male disciples that Jesus had indeed risen! Much has been written concerning the important role of women in the life of Jesus and the early church and how he brought them from a life of exile into the kingdom of God. I will make use of their encouragement and forge ahead with what I believe to be necessary for our time in history.

This story was energized by the firsthand experience of other women like myself, who have known marginalization, separation, and dismissal in the existing missionary world. The gifts and callings of women have lacked a voice; those who are considered too strong, too outside the mainstream of church culture, and whose lives have lacked the near perfection wanted by traditional mission societies. It is to that end that this study has been attempted.

My hope is that a small women's mission called Harvest Emergent Relief (HER) will serve as a forerunner mission that will take its strategic place together with others of like mind who are called to similar tasks. HER has the vision and indeed the opportunity to spearhead a fresh movement of women called to revisit the original ways of Jesus as people called to walk alongside and bring forth the kingdom of God. Not only is this long past due but it is critical for the days ahead. No longer is it church as usual, nor should it be. No longer is it missionary activity as usual, nor should it be. The times in which we live call not only for strategic thinking but consecrated, set apart, focus on the One we are following. At present there are many people, indeed countless women, who are not being utilized in their capacity and calling as radical lovers of God. I make the case, that to not place these women on the frontlines of missionary work is not only a mistake, it is a tragedy.

Acknowledgements

ALWAYS FIRST, I THANK the lover of my soul, the anchor of my heart, and the redeemer of my life, Jesus Christ, God of mercy. Thank you Elizabeth Glanville for your wisdom and faithfulness, Marguerite Schuster for your selflessness and care, Anne Tumility for your kindness and perseverance and Mark Labberton whose prayers and friendship have kept me afloat for many years.

For all who have given me great encouragement throughout the many seasons of my life, in particular I would like to thank: Thena and Ted Beam, Cherry Brandstater, Betty Sue Brewster, James Butler, Anne and Jose Calvo, Mary and David Dare, Stuart Dauermann, Jon and Sarah Dephouse, Bette Doiron, Susan Dow, Heather and Rick Engel, Dave Eubank, Jami Scotti Everett, Erik and Hayley Felten, Karin Finkler, Tracy Gary, David Gill, Mark Goeser, Thomas Howard, Lynne Hudson, Denise Kehrer, Santha Kumari, Lori McAlister, Paul and Cassie McCarty, Randy and Nicole Mc-Caskill, Karen Mulder, Doug Nason, Rebecca and Jose Nithi, Julie Nixon, Lisa Ravenhill, Shawn Redford, Randy Reese, Dave Rinker, Joe Roos, Wilbert Shenk, Jim Skillen, Carmen Valdes, Jim Wallis, Nancy Watters, Alan Weaver, Dudley Woodberry, Alyxius and Marcus Young and lastly, my co-pyeditor, Nancy Shoptaw and publisher Wipf and Stock, who encouraged me and believed in this project.

Thank you to Mother Clare, Sister Chiara, Mother Grace and the sisters of the Poor Clare Monastery in Santa Barbara, California. You showed me the love of Jesus Christ and him crucified. In so doing, you pointed me toward the life of a contemplative in action. Finally, I am forever grateful and remain indebted to Jackie Pullinger, Elizabeth Hynd, and Heidi Baker for showing me the heart of Jesus and the reality of a life lived in the power of the Holy Spirit.

Introduction

The Backstory

MY OWN PARTICULAR SEARCH for truth took many forms. I learned to ask the hard questions in the context of social justice issues. This framework was a natural progression from Marxism to increasingly more radical forms of feminism. I rummaged through every bottom line I could find. Nothing would satisfy my desire to know why things were the way they were.

In the late 1960s, my political activism increased as an awareness of racism drew me to the civil rights movement. As boys were dying and villages were being napalmed in Viet Nam I also became active in the anti-war movement. The first time I protested at the nation's capital, we heard that President Richard Nixon was standing at his window, looking down on us and laughing. I remember the cold wind blowing hard over the Potomac and I was determined that my voice would be heard as I joined a million others protesting the war.

As the war escalated, in the early 1970s I was introduced to Marxist-Leninist ideology, thought, and practice in my search for truth. Serious attempts were made to discern the times from a Marxist viewpoint. As radicalized women we formed cell groups and studied everything Marx, Lenin, Trotsky, and friends had to say about the causes of oppression in the world. The choices I made took on deeper meaning as I committed to fight for the poor, the marginalized, and the oppressed for the rest of my life.

Then something interesting began to happen. As strong activist women of the Marxist persuasion, we began to redefine the proletariat, and most of us walked away from the male-dominated Left. In the process, the new wave of the feminist movement was birthed. We began to form consciousness-raising groups, study groups, and strategic cell groups. We marched to take back the night, to take back our right to choose, and to take back our lives. For many of us, the deepening political study of the global oppression of women only catapulted us to the edges of radical separatism. We became a nation unto ourselves. I made decisions that threw me into the heart of the women's community. We had everything we needed: emotional, financial, physical, and strategic support. We were visionaries embracing the struggle. Festivals, conferences, restaurants, businesses, and strategy sessions fueled our hope and our determination.

For many years, this was who I was and what I fought for. In the early years of my participation in the civil rights movement, the anti-war movement, and the feminist movement, I found the exhilaration of solidarity against hatred, domination, and oppression profoundly fulfilling. What could be more important than fighting evil in all these forms? But I continued to dig and ask the basic philosophical questions. The questions mostly began with "Why?" Why did evil exist anyway? Why was there suffering and genocide? Marx saw the origins of evil in the collective choice of the *bourgeoisie*. But I wanted to know the whats and the hows and the whys of it all.

Many answers came to me at a place called L'Abri Fellowship in a small village in the Swiss Alps.[1] It was there in a snow-covered chalet that I originally came to Christ on the basis of epistemology, but that was not enough to hold my heart.[2] I returned to the US in greater pain than when I left. I knew the truth, but did not like it, as I continued to struggle with the face of the American church. No one seemed to care for the poor, and the women's movement was so misunderstood. I had come to Christ intellectually, but my heart was divided. I wrote an article called "Two Communities," and in it I compared the Christian community and the women's community.[3] I saw the one as having stale, sterile, cold truth and the other as having compas-

---

1. L'Abri Fellowship is located in Huémoz, a small village in the French Alps of Switzerland. Francis and Edith Schaeffer birthed the Christian community in the early 1970s. The community, which continues today in various countries, is focused on answering hard questions with honest answers.

2. Epistemology is "a branch of philosophy that investigates the origin, nature, methods, and limits to human knowledge." Primarily concerned with propositional knowledge, epistemology has been focused on propositional knowledge in discussion and determination of truth (*Random House Living Dictionary*, 2nd ed., s.v. "epistemology.")

3. Written in 1976; unpublished.

sionate, comforting, supportive love. I opted for the latter. Once again, I threw myself into radical political activity.

Part of the time I lived in Washington, DC, in a group house with other women committed to struggle and revolution. We knew our phones were tapped and that various government agencies were alert to our activities. We protested nuclear arms build-up often at the Pentagon. My sisters and I were committed to the struggle, and overthrowing the existing powers seemed to be the obvious answer. The problem was in how to do it.

We organized pro-choice rallies, anti-nuclear protests, and gay rights marches; if there was a protest, march, or rally, we probably organized it. I also worked with a radical feminist quarterly, developing political theory—strong minds struggling over mammoth issues of the day.

Many of us traveled back and forth between Washington, DC, and Berkeley for political as well as personal reasons. Involved in Women's Music (a genre of music birthed out of our feminist communities) we produced concerts, festivals, rallies, and sit-ins. The feminist movement was not only a growing political force and a dynamic community but it had a culture all of its own. We did not need anything. The personal and the political had merged.

The weight of social change, not to mention revolution, is a heavy load to carry. In the process of trying to change the society around us, we began to crumble internally. Many women made the decision to get clean and sober but we knew we needed a power greater than ourselves. In order to obtain spiritual power, some friends chose to be influenced by Hinduism or Buddhism, while others explored various emerging New Age beliefs. At this time some in the women's community were beginning to investigate goddess worship and adapting historical pagan worship to the feminist cause. A huge shift began and I became increasingly uncomfortable with the direction chosen. Not only was it not enough, it was in total contradiction to the truth I had found in Christianity. I may not have been living out the truth, but I knew where it could be found.

Duplicity in the movement began to show itself as the betrayal came to me both personally as well as politically. I was confronted with the cold hard fact that we in the radical feminist movement were doing to each other the same things that we were fighting against in the world. As it turned out, we were just as greedy and full of pride as the people we loathed. The realization and the hurt went deep. The movie *Reds* came out, and I identified with Emma Goldman as she stood in her freezing apartment in Moscow after fighting for revolution all of her life. She turned to Jack Reed and asked, "Is this what we have been fighting for?" I felt the same, knowing deep betrayal and faced with the realization that I had spent most of my life fighting for a cause that only had part of the truth. The foundation was not only unsteady; it was cracked at the base.

My life changed dramatically as I bought a one-way ticket to Hong Kong in search of the God from whom I had walked away, ridiculed, and denied. I was certain God would have nothing more to do with me, but I met Jesus in the bottom of a boat in the midst of a great storm in the South China Sea. But that is another story for another time.

As the years went by and I attempted to follow Christ, there were two main ways that the will of God was often made known to me: one was through scripture and the other through reading missionary biographies—the life stories of those pioneers who risked all they had and all they were to follow Jesus/Yeshua and bring the love of God to those who had never heard. They were examples of courage and relentless pursuit of God through intense suffering. The fire in my soul is continually stoked by the fact that these women chose to embrace the Cross rather than retreat.

The examples of sacrificial living from women like Gladys Aylward, Mildred Cable, Annie R. Taylor, Amy Carmichael, Dorothy Day, Jackie Pullinger, and others have helped to shape the mandate from God for many years now. I began to understand that my destiny was no longer to be a radical fighting against God but to be changed into a radical fighting for the kingdom of God on my knees. From there, I chose to go to the spiritually darkest places on the planet to rescue those who were without hope.

As I endeavored to navigate the waters of the missionary world, as someone having come from a radical background before I came to Christ, I was mostly met with lukewarm welcome and unspoken warning. There was more culture shock involved in entering the missionary world than there ever was working in countries overseas, including Tibet, India, and Burma.

While working in Bangkok with prostitutes and bouncers, the rather conservative missionary community did not think that a Christian woman should be staying out late at night, hanging with the needy in bars. I encountered much rejection as I tried to follow after Jesus in the ways I felt I was being led. I attempted to join different mission organizations until finally God pulled me up short and made it clear that I must not compare myself to others. I must not try to be accepted in a missionary agency just because almost everyone else did. God gave me the scripture John 21:21–22. Peter is asking Yeshua/Jesus, "What about him?" (referring to John) and Jesus says, "What is that to you; you follow Me." This story is important to me because I knew that I was being asked to walk alone with Jesus. God would be enough for me!

In one sense my story is comprised of various levels of exile, some chosen, some forced upon me, and some directed by God. My heart was always drawn to work with people who lived and worked on the margins, either physically or philosophically. My own background is part of what has led to the writing of this book.

The Reason for Pursuit

There is need for a momentum shift in missiological thinking and there is a desperate need for a women's mission, which could lead the way to a women's missionary movement. The emergence of such a mission is indeed fraught with skepticism from many of those inside the church; and a women's missionary movement is not on the minds of leaders in the missionary world.

It is my belief that the heart of God is looking for women whom the church and missionary world deem unfit for service among the lost. Whether the existing Christian organizational "powers" can see these women is another question. This study will take the reader on a journey from skepticism and suspicion to one of welcome not only for the lost of this world but also for the marginalized women in the body of Christ that still linger "outside the [church] gate."

This study's passion is found in the belief that radicalized women everywhere are sidelined from ministry functions within the body of Christ. The phrase "radicalized women" is understood as those women who have been pushed to the edges of the church as well as society, either because of choice, failure, or common missionary tradition. They are women who have already counted the cost and have made the decision to follow Christ without the need for being "released" by men or mission societies. Many have such strong pioneering calls on their lives that unless they are galvanized toward following Christ, they will turn and use their gifts elsewhere.

Because of many of these women's backgrounds or lifestyles before their encounter with Yeshua/Jesus, the church remains skeptical as to their allegiance. Others are seen as stumbling too many times after coming to Christ and have never found forgiveness in the church. Nevertheless, they resolve to walk with Jesus outside the institutional church, where others who do not know Jesus are floundering either in anger or despair. For these women the road is filled with landmines, but they know they must go to Jesus "outside the camp" because that is where God is to be found (Heb 13:12–13).

The importance of exile is undergirded by the fact that not only did many of the prophetic voices in scripture experience exile or separation in one form or another, but also that Christian history is littered with examples of exile being part of God's intimate formation of individuals and communities. The discovery of exile in the lives of these pioneering women missionaries has been prominent and points to the strategic ways God uses exile in the lives of these believers.

One of the reasons for writing this book is to send a message to those in power, as well as to gather those who will help build a women's mission and hopefully spark a movement where women of like mind can work side by side in order to fight for those who are oppressed. Women who are walking in weakness and brokenness and who are unashamed are an invitation for the healing power and purpose of God to be made manifest. This is a movement of women willing to say:

> For I determined to know nothing among you except Jesus Christ and him crucified. I was with you in weakness and much trembling, and my message and my preaching were not in persuasive words of wisdom, but in demonstration of the Spirit and of power. (1 Cor 2:2–4)

This book is but one step in discovering a way to reach those whom the missionary world considers unreachable, untouchable, or undesirable, to penetrate the places of most resistance with the welcoming words of the gospel of Jesus. Briefly put, the goal is to bring forth the kingdom of God out on the edge as some have been uniquely designed to do. My prayer is that a unique women's mission will be faithful to proclaim the gospel to this generation without compromise and without negligence, and to preach the Cross in the power of the Holy Spirit so that redemption might come to many. This is my goal, my prayer; and in God's mercy, just maybe a handful of converted radical women will be the catalytic force to bring forth a twenty-first-century women's missionary movement.

There are many parts to this puzzle and yet I do not know of anyone working in this area. Hopefully, new ground will be broken and options offered to those women who think they have no choice in how to follow

Jesus. It is possible that the creation of a women's mission could be one of the missing pieces that will help enable the spreading of the gospel and bring forth the kingdom of God in this slice of history.

Then the Lord answered me and said:

> Write the vision;
> make it plain on tablets,
> so that a runner may read it. (Hab 2:2)

PART I

Scaffolding

Exile is an image that might enlighten us concerning the truth of our status anywhere, at any time—aliens, wanderers, . . .

There is no hope in government; the hope is in exiles.

ELIZABETH MCALISTER, JONAH HOUSE

ONE

Navigation

THE CENTRAL ISSUE OF this study has been to identify aspects of exile that have shaped selected pioneering women and their contribution to Christian missions. The overview includes: how exile is defined, how exile has shaped the life and mission of both historical and present-day pioneering women missionaries, how the construction of a new hermeneutic is critical, and how to apply this hermeneutic to create a women's mission and movement.

The significance of this book can be stated in three parts: personal, organizational, and missiological. My personal desire is to bring radical women who ardently oppose Christianity to deep conversion and out of that, the emergence of a new mission and movement of truly radicalized women.

In terms of organizational importance, beginning with the creation of a specifically prepared women's mission, I would like to see a ground swell that at some point will grow into small communities. I propose that Harvest Emergent Relief (HER), a forerunner mission, serve as an example and prototype of what would help to bring a new understanding of what is required in the years ahead.

Missiological impact can be found in the hope that radicalized women will become collaborators in a new surge of subversive Christian activity. Missiologists can gain prophetic insight as they bring an understanding of those women who are outside the missionary community, indeed outside of the church. When these women find their destiny in following Jesus/Yeshua, the significance of a new women's mission will be evident.

Because I am choosing to focus on women in pioneering situations, I do not discuss: (1) men's involvement in the formation of a women's mission; (2) women who are recruited by missionary organizations and fit easily into the existing mission groups; and (3) women who are involved in normative missionary work and not pioneering endeavors.

The following words are used throughout the book and therefore definitions seem necessary in order to benefit the reader. *Radical* is the word that most aptly describes the kind of women who are drawn to high-risk areas. It is a word that implies the capacity to go to the root, the *radix*, the beginning point. Radicalization has to do with intrinsic transformation, to recover the intended meaning of an idea, person, or movement. A radical is someone who believes deeply and holds strong convictions. A radical is typically one who seeks to get to the bottom of things and turn perspectives upside down in order to change a set of assumptions, ideas, or situations (see Acts 17:6).

Hermeneutic is defined as "the art or science of interpretation."[1] The word is often used in the area of biblical interpretation, but it is also used in the discipline of philosophy. I am using the word hermeneutic in order to impress upon the reader a broader range of vision, a deeper look at how one views reality—a substantive paradigm shift. This applies to the missional context and also to the church.[2]

Crucible is "a severe test or trial, esp. one that causes a lasting change or influence."[3] The *American Heritage Dictionary* defines crucible "as a place, time or situation characterized by the confluence of powerful intellectual, social, economic or political forces; a severe test of patience or belief; a vessel for melting material at high temperatures."[4]

In Part I I describe the mechanics and particulars of my research. This part explains the methodology, hermeneutical understanding, and theories that are employed. Social movement theory and exile theory are used for a deeper comprehension of the dynamics of justice movements. Both are necessary in order to understand the heart of this new women's mission.

Frames and lenses bring into focus the grid through which reality is interpreted. The social movement frame and the political subframe have been chosen to showcase the subject at hand. Gender bias is included as a

1. *Random House Webster's College Dictionary*, 3rd ed., s.v. "hermeneutic."
2. Westphal, *Whose Community?*
3. *Random House Webster's College Dictionary*, 3rd ed., s.v. "crucible."
4. *American Heritage Dictionary*, 5th ed., s.v. "crucible."

lens because it is always present in dealing with life in a fallen world. The importance and therefore the discussion of exile threads its way through the chapters as the frames expose God's purposes through a life lived in exile.

Part II is an extensive roadmap that traverses the landscape of exile in order to give the reader a broader perspective. Different meanings and descriptions of exile are discussed, which show how God leverages a life lived in exile and how this can be used as a prophetic statement/witness/lifestyle.

The concept of exile builds on a scriptural foundation as it helps to explain the thinking of some on the inside of missional organizations and explores ways in which outsider observation can be an asset to one's walk with God in pioneering work. This in turn produces a way of seeing what is lacking in much of the church, the wider body of Christ.

Part II also looks at the emergence of social movements. Much of the change brought about in society takes place through consensus and conflict movements. Consideration of these two approaches help the reader to better understand the inauguration of a women's mission with implications for a broader movement. A fresh way of perceiving and approaching missions is set forth. Social movements because of their nature contain aspects of exile, and these are also discussed.

Part III gives the historical context from which the lives of pioneering women missionaries were shaped and how exile played a part. A basic narrative of specific historic and contemporary women missionaries follows, and shows how exile was instrumental in equipping these women to spread the gospel.

We look at two historical movements, each started by a handful of women, each important in its own way. The first is the fourth-century desert movement usually associated with the Desert Fathers. But often overlooked are the Desert Mothers, the first women's movement, which I have chosen to highlight here. The second is the women's missionary movement in the late nineteenth and early twentieth century. Because of the scope of this study I do not go into depth in this area, but touch on main points and momentum. Reasons for the movement's beginning, the argument of rights, and the outcome of each movement are discussed. A case is made for what these movements can teach, as we focus on the development of a women's mission and reflect on what is needed today.

The last sections of Part III focus on historical pioneering missionaries and the ways in which crucible events and exile shaped their lives. We then explore the lives of modern-day pioneering women, explaining the aspects of exile in their lives. I interviewed twenty-two missionary women, including sending questionnaires to those in hard-to-access countries. Narratives of specific women missionaries both historical and contemporary are used.

Part IV brings theory and practice together by discussing the implications of a women's mission. I attempt to answer unspoken objections with a challenge. I then probe the benefits and hindrances of a life lived in exile. The next section is divided into two segments: (1) the mission community of Harvest Emergent Relief (HER); and (2) the movement, which involves development of a new default culture and the momentum necessary for growth. The development of this culture is given language by creating a friaristic focus.

First, I discuss using HER as a prototype, showing how different mission groups are gauged and what leadership looks like in the trenches of high-risk areas of involvement, such as war zones, refugee camps, and aiding Internally Displaced Persons (IDPs). This chapter concludes with considering strategic areas of involvement on the borderlands of nations in conflict, showing how women of exile who are formed into a mission of their own can bring needed change.

The conclusion is an attempt to cast the vision and show why the times in which we live cry out for a new way of seeing missiologically. The need for a new hermeneutic must be considered if a change in missiological thinking is to take place. My greater hope is that a women's mission will serve as a type of forerunner mission-community that will take its strategic place together with others engaged in similar tasks. My prayer is that this new women's mission will usher in a women's missionary movement. My endeavor is to explain why radicalized women who come from outside the church, as well as inside the missionary community are ready to take their place in the *missio Dei*.

Two

Frames, Lens, and Theory

THIS CHAPTER DESCRIBES THE foundational steppingstones for creating a women's mission and community. Although I assumed there would be a plethora of writing and information available on the topic, this was not the case. In the primary area of exile, I drew upon different categories of approach and groupings including exilic texts in scripture, tradition of exile in the ascetic movement, insider/outsider thinking, historical protest movements, women's movements and women in exile, as well as artists and writers in exile.

The insider mentality and outsider interpretation found in scripture was a necessary starting point in terms of understanding the dynamics of women missionaries in general and pioneering women in particular. I found very little written from this particular slant. Much of the understanding came through the reading of topics not necessarily focused on but implied within insider and outsider thinking. To aid in my research, I conducted interviews and perused archives.

This in turn led me to investigate the lives of women in mission history, and women's missionary movements, as well as social movements in general.

Historical Biographical Research

The literature reviewed for the historical section is anything but plentiful, yet I did find information from Laura Swan, Patricia Ranft, Mary T. Malone, Diana Butler Bass, and others regarding the Desert Mothers of the fourth century. In the words of Mary Malone, referring to male historians' approach to including women in their references, "All historical observations about women remain partial, distorted, eccentric and ultimately profoundly dissatisfying. We are left with fragments and each historian has to cobble together a credible story from such pitiably sparse remains."[1] This is sadly true when investigating the lives of the Desert Mothers.

Digging through old manuscripts, biographies, and autobiographies was vital in order to discover what women missionaries of the past had experienced. The nature of my research required that I glean from scarce writings in the historical pioneering women's chapters of archival sources as well as books from my own personal missionary book collection.

I found great value in looking at literature from the original women's missionary movement and then comparing it to the possibilities of a new movement emerging. Historical findings regarding the first women's missionary movement led to interesting resources. Dana L. Robert and Ruth A. Tucker bring a wealth of scholarly work to the table. Robert has written books having to do with American women in mission and Christian mission in general with specific focus on women. Tucker is well known for her historical work on women in the missionary world.

Helen Barrett Montgomery, missiologist and ordained preacher, gives a remarkable account of the women's missionary movement. One of the many books she wrote was called, *Western Women in Eastern Lands*, dated 1910. In it she documents the history of the women's missionary movement. In 1924, Montgomery's translation of *The New Testament in Modern English* was published. Her friendship with Susan B. Anthony, crusader for women's rights will be discussed later.

Field Research

I chose to interview Christian women missionaries from various backgrounds, living in either dangerous situations or hard-to-access countries. The twenty-two women were presented with fifty-seven questions and they responded in numerous ways; some giving more substantive answers than others. Because of the nature and geographical location of their work, out of necessity I have not given their real names.

Interviews were conducted and questionnaires were sent via email, and in some instances telephone conversations were used to obtain the

1. Malone, *Women and Christianity*, 246.

necessary data. Because those interviewed worked in many countries, comparing their experiences was complicated. One of the main obstacles is that these women are presently in situations where it is not easy to communicate, much less conduct follow-up interviews in person. For example, one woman is living in Tibet among nomads, three others are in the jungles of Burma, and still others are hidden in China. (Categories of the interviews for contemporary women missionaries can be found in appendix A.) The questions asked early on in the interview provide the story from which exile was acted out in each woman's life.

Frames and Lens for Understanding

Frames are used to build an understanding of the way one perceives life. As I worked my way through these particular frames of understanding, I began to see the possibility of creating an expanded reality for those who do not have the vision for this new kind of mission.

Using a camera as an illustration, the main frame chosen was social justice, with the political subframe bringing it into focus. The social justice frame is used as the basis for interpreting the collective angst of people whose lives have been altered and indeed quashed due to discrimination and inequity. The lack of impartiality on the part of those in positions of power has left an indelible mark on the spirits of those committed to righting the wrongs not only in their personal lives but in society as a whole.

The political subframe works well with the exile and social movement theories that are developed. This subframe is necessary because not only are there situations where a women's mission will be working in politically precarious situations at best, but the inner workings of the community itself will have political components which will be ongoing issues.

Deeper understanding of the frames comes when seen through the lens of gender bias. Both the frames and lens that I have chosen to use accentuate the intricacies of leadership by bringing knowledge and passion together. This blend gives a more complete picture and added perspective. Both of these frames and the gender-bias lens are looked at closely and used as tools for analysis.

Social Justice Frame

Discussion on the various approaches of looking at social justice as a frame is found in the book, *Frames of Protest* by Hank Johnston and John A. Noakes. They make the comment, "At its most basic, a frame identifies a problem that is social or political in nature, the parties responsible for causing the problem, and a solution."[2]

The social justice frame has been adjusted to accommodate a new way of looking at collective action, such as the formation of a women's mission with implications for a later movement surge. Johnston and Noakes make the point that frames are always evolving and therefore cannot be held hostage to the initial way they were created or used.[3] There are frames within frames, and also what are known as breaking frames.

Another way to look at frames is to see that there are usually "competing frames."[4] For example, in this study I identify the traditional missionary community as being one frame and those who would question it as having their own frames. Frames have basic subjective components and are perceptions of what is happening.

Johnston and Noakes go on to highlight David A. Snow and Robert D. Benford, social movement theorists, and explain the three fundamental framing tasks as they see it.[5] The tasks are useful for explaining the issue at hand.

- *Diagnostic framing* presents to potential recruits a new interpretation of issues or events; like a medical diagnosis, it tells what is wrong and why.

- *Prognostic framing* presents a solution to the problem suggested in the diagnosis.

- *Motivational framing* attempts to present to people a reason to join collective action—the problem defined in the diagnosis and the solution in the prognosis are usually not sufficient to get people to act.[6]

For our purposes here I would describe framing in the following ways. The *diagnostic framing* shows the problem as being one of exclusion and

---

2. Johnston and Noakes, *Frames of Protest*, 5.
3. Ibid., 16.
4. Ibid.
5. Ibid., 5–6; see pp. 1–29 for more information on the fundamental framing tasks.
6. Ibid., 5.

exile due to gender bias in the missionary community and illustrates the lack of initiative to include those women who have been sidelined for one reason or another and therefore have experienced various types of individual exile. The *prognostic framing* gives a solution by forming a women's mission in order to exercise the giftings and callings of those particular women. Creating a collective action community will bring women of exile together. The *motivational framing* challenges women to go to places of high risk and danger in their worship, prayer, and action. A women's mission would be a way of coming together out of exile in order to fight for justice in many forms and to glorify God in the hard places of ministry where injustice runs rampant.

The understanding of "justice" can be used in a variety of ways depending on the context. The term "social justice" brings in the dimension of societal concern and with it a certain degree of latitude. Rose Marie Berger, editor and writer for *Sojourners Magazine*, says, "Justice is the moral code that guides a fair and equitable society. When an individual acts on behalf of justice, he or she stands up for what is right."[7]

That moral code encompasses economic, social, legal, and personal areas.

Berger goes on to say:

> Social justice issues are determined by "discerning the signs of the times" (Matthew 16:3), a careful process of social analysis. First, we listen to and observe the experiences of those closest to the problem. Second, together with those closest to the problem, we look at the context. What's the history and what are the root causes? Are there political and/or cultural forces at play? We take the expanded information (experience plus context) and examine it in light of biblical values and Christian teaching. What would Jesus do in a situation like this? Third, we ask: What action might successfully make this situation more just? Finally, we take the

---

7. Berger, "What the Heck is 'Social Justice'"?, 37. Rose Marie Berger is a poet, community organizer, and social activist, as well as being an editor and writer for *Sojourners Magazine*. Sojourners is a community of people who are committed to engaging in social justice issues from a biblical perspective. They started out in Chicago in the early 1970s and later moved to Washington, DC. The *Sojourners Magazine* was a natural outgrowth of their lives together. It has now become a non-profit and continues to be a prophetic voice in the body of Christ. Berger's book *Who Killed Donte Manning?* was published in 2010 and I highly recommend it for understanding the outworkings of justice.

action and evaluate the results. The evaluation takes us back to step one.[8]

The working definition of justice being used in the context of this book is not only the equal treatment of women in the missionary world, the Christian world, and the world at large, it is the intervention in the face of evil to rescue those who are being oppressed. These oppressive political issues come in the form of trafficking, economic disparity, tyrannical governments, rape used as a weapon of war, abandonment, children forced to become soldiers, and the list goes on. The oppression is the relentless ideological rant of a few over the well being of the many. Because evil is systemic in nature, it must be dealt with on that level, as well as on the ground where rescue and compassion reach out to those who are held captive. Social justice is the outworking of a person committed to walking with God. Micah 6:8 says it well:

> He has told you, O mortal, what is good; and what does the Lord require of you, but to do justice, and love kindness and to walk humbly with your God?

Miroslav Volf in his book, *Exclusion and Embrace*, comments on Gustavo Gutierrez's *A Theology of Liberation*, saying, "Doing justice, struggling against injustice, was not an optional extra of Israelite faith. To know God is to do justice."[9] I would add that to know God is to bring into community those who have known exile; this too is doing justice.

Fighting against the evil of apartheid, Annemie Bosch, (along with her late husband, missiologist David Bosch[10]) from South Africa, says this about injustice:

> When two opposing forces clash and somebody steps in between them to seek reconciliation, the reconciler often gets crushed. This is what happened to Jesus. This is what the cross is all about. If we, like Jesus, seek first God's kingdom and justice, and if we choose to join Jesus in the ministry of reconciliation, there is no escape from the cross. In the way of Jesus, only the willingness to suffer

8. Ibid.

9. Volf, *Exclusion and Embrace*, 217.

10. Professor of Missiology at the University of South Africa, Pretoria, David Bosch's influence on and contribution to mission studies is enormous. His early work, *Witness to the World* was followed by his groundbreaking, *Transforming Mission*.

injustice can overcome injustice, and only compassion can move us to suffer to ease the suffering of others.[11]

Annemie Bosch talks about integrity, safety and weakness.

> If due to fear of circumstances, we hold our tongue and don't speak up for justice, we lose our sense of integrity. We allow our torment-ers to hold us hostage emotionally, and we trade our integrity for safety. As a result, we are often filled with a kind of self-reproach. If, on the other hand, we lose ourselves in God and in the cause we are fighting for, our flagging hope and courage will be rekindled, "for if we are weak, then we are strong."[12]

When facing injustice as our mission is called to do, there must always be present the humility that keeps us from bitterness of soul. It is not hard to become jaded and rancorous when confronted on a consistent basis with evil in its many configurations. Sometimes that takes the form of power dynamics, both within and without. This leads us to the political subframe.

Political Subframe

The *political subframe* lends the best traction for understanding the dynam-ics in play. The political has to do with power and domination. In the early days of the second wave of the feminist movement, there was a saying: "The personal is political and the political is personal." This means that the political actions and ideas come from the personal lives of women; they revolve around the personal and wash over our intimate lives. It meant con-siderably more back in the early movement days, but for the purposes here, that is all that needs to be said.

Many books have been written on the politics of Jesus, including those by the Daniel Berrigan and Philip Berrigan, Elizabeth McAlister, John Howard Yoder, Jim Wallis, and Obrey M. Hendricks.[13] Much of what they say brings prophetic insight into our present situation. Hendricks, for

11. A. Bosch, "Suffering for Justice," 216.

12. Ibid., 222.

13. John Howard Yoder (1927–1997) was a Mennonite who was best known for his stand on pacifism. He was a Christian scholar focused on theology and ethics. Jim Wallis is best known as the founder of Sojourner's Community in Washington, DC. He is the author of numerous books and continues to be a prophetic voice in the public square. Obery M. Hendricks is a professor at New York Theological Seminary, where he teaches in the area of biblical interpretation.

example, talks about the politics of Jesus and says, "The principles of Jesus' politics are rooted in the most foundational ethics of the Bible." He highlights three along with their Hebrew word: (1) *mishpat*/justice; (2) *sadiqah*/righteousness; and (3) *hesed*/steadfast love.[14] Jesus not only embodied these when he came from heaven and lived on earth, but Jesus is true justice, real righteousness, and unwavering steadfast love. This is the very character of God; it is immutable and cannot change.

Nicholas Winter, in his book, *Dangerous Frames,* discusses the not so subtle experiences of those who are affected by injustice of various kinds but also the hidden component that comes into play in political and public discourse. Winter develops a theory of "group implication" in which he describes issues being crafted in order to match the desired results by transferring back the preferred response.[15] Winter goes on to make the case that the outcome of injustice is the radicalization of those being oppressed in one form or another.

The political subframe helps to understand the volatile situations in each region where the women will be serving. The care that we take within each country or region or area of conflict is the same kind of care that we will take in our relationships with each other in our community. Ongoing interaction is critical for each person to be able to respond with trust and integrity as community is built. Because the main political issue is power, no matter what scenario, be it individual or geographic, community or country, the guiding rule will be intentionally waiting on God.

Political power can be a good thing if it is used correctly; but if it is unjust and oppressive it can be the conduit for selfishness and arrogance. Our values, ethics, and strategies must be grounded in a real humility that does not engage the wrong use of power. Our women all have leadership capacity, and as leaders they must grapple with power issues. They come from varied cultures and have different forms of ministry experiences. Most have strong giftings and have overcome all kinds of adversity to survive. They have experienced rejection for a number of reasons, one of which is being female in the typically male-dominated structure of the missionary world. So, the personal/political dynamics are important not only in treacherous situations but also in community life.

14. Hendricks, *Politics of Jesus,* 320.
15. Winter, *Dangerous Frames,* 31.

The Lens of Gender Bias

Gender bias is the lens I have chosen to use because it permeates all other frames. Race, class, and gender would normally be used as triangulating frames, but using gender bias as the lens will help to identify the issues. Because gender bias not only runs through race and class, it is usually the last element to be considered. But it is foundational for understanding attitudes and actions within the social justice frame, regarding women, mission, and movement. "Although there have been numerous battles over class, race and nation during the past three thousand years, none has brought the liberation of women."[16] Basically, "sexism is the root of all oppression."[17] Because of that, exile has often scarred women's lives. Jacqueline Rhodes has this to say in agreement: "The first foundational oppression in human history was sexism."[18] I would amend those statements as a Christian and say, that yes, sexism/gender bias is at the root of oppression, and yes, the first oppression in history was sexism but the root itself is the Fall. Further discussion on this topic is for another book.

The three lenses of *race, class,* and *gender* are complex layers of how we deal with life. Everything spins through these three filters. Each one influences the other but *gender* cuts through both race and class. After all of the justice issues have been dealt with concerning race and class, we are still left with the most fundamental issue of all: gender bias.

Gender bias or sexism is the most basic of all issues, especially as it influences the missionary world. Therefore, it is critical that we develop theories and projects with essential understanding of how gender plays a foundational role in our worldview and thus our decision making. It is important that we understand how we perceive gender. "All women are oppressed, but there is tremendous variety in the forms oppression takes and consequently in the strengths and weaknesses of our self-concepts."[19]

My research shows that exile still plays a large part in the makeup of gender bias issues in the missionary world. A woman acutely feels the separation and isolation when she is excluded from ministering in non-traditional ways and from decision making in male-defined and male-led mission organizations. But the prospect of repenting of gender bias has the

16. Bunch, *Passionate Politics*, 163.

17. Ibid.

18. Rhodes, *Radical Feminism*, 29.

19. Bunch, *Passionate Politics*, 85.

potential to change mission history. Repentance and then action brings the possibility of seeing a new women's mission come into being. This would be a true paradigm shift for those who have not chosen to see beyond the seen and would draw many women to labor together and leave the individual exile behind. Radical women that traditional missionary organizations have queries about will be able to take their place in the body of Christ and contribute in significant ways for growing the kingdom of God.

For example, in refugee camps like Darfur, where Muslim women are pushed to the back edges of the camps and are not given access to food or medicine, radicalized women who are not afraid of the consequences of their actions, as they are being led by the Holy Spirit, will be able to minister to these outsider women. Women involved in a new women's mission will have the ability to meet needs in dangerous situations where men are not qualified or able to participate.

Fighting gender bias through collective action is part of the calling of a women's mission and sets a strong example of how to bring about gender justice. Faith in God shows itself to be real when it works itself out by advocating for justice on behalf of those who cannot fight for themselves. I will give examples of this on the pages to come. For now, it is enough to say that this is the main thrust of a women's mission and of Harvest Emergent Relief in particular.

Hermeneutical Understanding

A greater hermeneutical understanding opens the door for a wider look at the potential problem the traditional missionary community might have, not only with the radicalized women themselves but with the creation of a women's mission. The exploration of philosophical hermeneutics gives language to the women who are marginalized missionaries or pre-missionaries, gives robust expression to the formation of a new women's mission, and lastly, gives language for discussion by existing missionary organizations.

Hermeneutics is normally used in conjunction with the biblical understanding of the text. But there is a wider meaning in the area of philosophical hermeneutics. "The hermeneutical has to do with bridging the gap between the familiar world in which we stand and the strange meaning that resists assimilation into the horizons of our world."[20] In other words, I am

20. Gadamer, *Philosophical Hermeneutics*, xii. Hans-Georg Gadamer was a German philosopher (1900–2002) and was the main proponent of philosophical hermeneutics.

using philosophical hermeneutics as a way to lessen the distance between what is understood to be proper protocol in the admission of women into a particular mission and those whose lives before they came to Christ prohibit acceptance in traditional organizations. Philosophical hermeneutics is primarily concerned with dialogue and what is necessary if we are to lessen the distance.

Hans-Georg Gadamer "redefines hermeneutics as 'the art of understanding.'"[21] For my purposes in this study, the experience of alienation has the potential to bring awareness to the missionary world at large and gives language to those who have been exiled and are looking at the situation as outsiders. The point is making the choice to understand. "The principle of hermeneutics simply means that we should try to understand everything that can be understood."[22] Another way of saying it, quoting Gadamer again, "The hermeneutical problem only emerges clearly when there is no powerful tradition present to absorb one's own attitude into itself and when one is aware of confronting an alien tradition to which he (sic) has never belonged or one he (sic) no longer unquestioningly accepts."[23]

The hermeneutical problem as it relates to the missionary community is that there is no prevailing tradition that is seen as viable for women who have been told or believe they do not fit in the schema of missionary activity. Those in mainline leadership positions do not accept these women. Established missionary organizations often have a limited understanding regarding missional concepts or definitions of who should be doing mission work, if women should be leading, or if women should be working in high-risk areas. The lack of vocabulary and of discernment lends little understanding of how best to engage women who are outsiders.

Coming to the table with open minds and willing hearts determined to dialogue is essential. The key words are *dialogue* and *understanding*. We must ask the hard questions and be willing to lay aside our current perceptions and perhaps see in a new way. We must also be willing to question what has come before and approach the horizon with new eyes. Gadamer talks about the fusion of two horizons, the dialectic of give and take; they

---

He gained much from the insight of Martin Heidegger. To learn more about his life, a biography has been written by Jean Grondin, *Hans-Georg Gadamer*. His most well known book is *Truth and Method* (1960).

21. Thiselton, *Hermeneutics*, 3.

22. Gadamer, *Philosophical Hermeneutics*, 31.

23. Ibid., 46; see also Laughery, *Living Hermeneutics in Motion*.

are needed to understand one another. This fusing need not be a collision, as some would believe, but more of an emerging, a melding together, a blending of the old and the new with our goal being the same: the preaching of the gospel to the ends of the earth. Prophetic dialogue is what is needed at this table of generosity, knowing that God is present and the Holy Spirit is longing to speak if we will but listen.

I make a case that there must be an adjustment in our hermeneutical understanding so that transformation in our thinking might take place and there be a fresh way of living out our missiological calling. Much tradition is good and right and true, but we must not be held captive by antiquated and worn out ways of perceiving the best way to go about our common goal. The possibility of going in a new direction is a risk worth taking, indeed it is fundamental risk that is necessary and we must come together in dialogue to begin the process.

Theory

For my study, both exile theory and social movement theory were chosen because they help to distill a new understanding of the effect of exile in the missionary women that we focus on. I amend the two specific theories as I draw on both to not only complement but also construct fresh ideas, which should be of benefit to the larger missionary community. The theoretical frameworks of exile and social movements bring into focus the themes of exile, godly leverage, and insider/outsider thinking.

What is the best way to do this? I have been looking at the lives of historical pioneering women missionaries: the ways in which they lived, what they fought for, what they experienced, their life of faith, and the God they knew, and comparing them with the lives of contemporary pioneering missionaries. From this I extract the essence of what the pioneering life of a woman looks like and how that affects the possibility of a women's mission and movement.

Exile Theory

Charlotte Bunch, feminist activist and theorist, says, "Theory is not something set apart from our lives. Our assumptions about reality and change influence our actions constantly. The question is not whether we have a theory, but how aware we are of the assumptions behind our actions, and how conscious we are of the choices we make daily among different theories."[24] Bunch developed her own model of theory and structured it into four parts:

- *Description:* Describing what exists . . .

- *Analysis:* Analyzing why that reality exists . . .

- *Vision:* Determining what should exist . . .

- *Strategy:* Hypothesizing how to change what is to what should be . . .[25]

This model will be adapted for the development of a theory of exile. I describe what exile looks like, analyzing what that means in the grand scheme of things, casting a vision in order to determine what should exist, and lastly, looking at strategy.

The theoretical foundation for exile comes from the belief that, on some level, in some form, exile is an ingredient in the lives of those passionately pursuing deeper ways of understanding and being. They are complex and difficult to explain, therefore I have expanded the common use of the word exile to include not only separation from one's own country but also inner, political, spiritual, emotional, and ideological spheres of exile. In one sense this is an attempt to refocus the usual parameters of the understanding of the word exile.

Walter Brueggemann wanted to "tilt the metaphor of exile" and says, "exile is not primarily geographical, but it is social, moral and cultural."[26] James H. Houston believes that exiles are those that "move away from the familiar and the conventional and into the dangerously exposed places, to prophetically critique our cultural norms and institutional norms."[27] For my purposes, the theory of exile emanates from one major premise: that exile plays a significant role in the lives of those who call themselves followers of Jesus Christ.

My theory of exile is in the context of the missionary world, the church at large, and the pioneering women missionaries with whom I have studied and interviewed. Above all this it is a practical theory. A more extensive look at the description and meaning of exile will be addressed in Part II: Exile as a Road Map.

24. Bunch, *Passionate Politics*, 243.

25. Ibid., 244–45.

26. Brueggemann, *Cadences of Home*, 2.

27. Houston, *Joyful Exiles*, 12.

Social Movement Theory

Social Movement Theory analysts attempt to explain why movements occur, what mobilizes them, and what the outcomes are in the long run. Many of their ideas come from examples of the anti-war movement, the civil rights movement, the feminist movement, the gay rights movement, and the lesbian-feminist movement. I draw on some of their thinking to help validate the need for a radicalized women's mission.

When looking at social movement theory regarding the radical feminist movement there were errors in judgment and/or application by proponents of the theory. For the most part, the error had to do with what was truly the focus during the second wave of the feminist movement beginning in the 1960s and 1970s. Having said that, the choice was made to take from social movement theory what was good, necessary, and expedient.

Charles Tilly and Lesley J. Wood, key proponents of social movement theory, make the statement, "By the twenty-first century, people all over the world recognized the term 'social movement' as a trumpet call, as a counterweight to oppressive power, as a summons to popular action against a wide range of scourges."[28]

My working definition of social movements, based on my reading and life experience, is that they are made up of individuals or groups brought together because of dissatisfaction, grievance, marginalization, collective consciousness, or ideology in order to challenge the prevailing understanding and/or structure needing transformation. Social movements are primarily concerned with social change. They ebb and flow depending on the historical setting.

For example, the feminist movement that surged again in the 1960s was made up of different factions or concerns but they were all considered part of the movement as a whole. There was everything from more conservative organizations like NOW (National Organization for Women) on one end of the spectrum, to the lesbian-separatist contingency on the other, with many groups in-between. They were strengthened by numerous cell groups and individuals developing feminist political theory, engaging in social concerns in various camps, as well as cultivating a new culture of their own. The spectrum of the women's community spanned music, politics, philanthropy, medicine, education, spirituality, and so on.

---

28. Tilly and Wood, *Social Movements*, 3.

Some of the current social movement theory is not flexible enough to understand movements such as the radical feminist movement or a women's missionary movement. Luther P. Gerlach and Virginia H. Hine present their understanding of social movements in a clear way as they define a movement as:

> A group of people who are organized for, ideologically motivated by, and committed to a purpose which implements some form of personal or social change; who are directly engaged in the recruitment of others; and whose influence is spreading in opposition to the established order within which it originated.[29]

Understanding social movements is not something only social scientists can learn from but also those who work for social change from the grassroots level. There is much to learn from social movements as it pertains to building a women's mission for radicalized women. Social movements also reveal why it is necessary for mission organizations to develop a fresh hermeneutic.

When considering how aspects of social movement theory might apply, the following assumptions are used:

- Every social movement begins with a small group.
- Every group begins with one visionary person.

These particular radicalized women live primarily on what some in the body of Christ would call the margins or outside the mainstream. But many of them are leaders in the world as we know it—politics, business, social justice advocacy, philanthropy, music industry, education, the arts, and so on—and yet the church views them as outsiders. I see redemptive gifts not being used and there is no one reaching out to these women, only protesting against them. When gifting is not used within the body of Christ, it will be exercised elsewhere.

Because these women are found in places like the feminist movement, gay rights movement, ongoing civil rights movement, and so on, the decision was made to use social movement theory as a tool. The women's involvement in other social movements is a precursor to envisioning the empowering of women in the realm of missions. The whole theory has not been embraced but what is can be a powerful backdrop for women to engage "the powers" with this time-worn path of true discipleship.

---

29. Gerlach and Hine, *People, Power, Change Movements*, xvi.

A movement of missional women will be made up of yielded, radical, destabilizing, delightful, disruptive, joy-filled disciples of Jesus. They will have their eyes fixed on Jesus to be led in only the ways that he can lead. Walter Brueggemann talks about hope, mission, and activism when he says, "Action is the risky engagement in a concrete bodily way—powered by hope, shaped by missional imagination—in order to make a difference in the world, to reconfigure the interplay between God's intention and the reality of the world."[30]

Without action, repentance is empty and God has no name.

---

30. Brueggemann, *Truth-Telling as Subversive Obedience*, 31.

PART II

Exile as a Roadmap

Do you continue to go with Jesus?
the way lies through Gethsemane,
through the city gate, outside the camp;
the way lies alone, and the way lies until
there is no trace of a footstep left,
only the voice, "Follow Me."

OSWALD CHAMBERS
MY UTMOST FOR HIS HIGHEST

THREE

Understandings of Exile

THREADS OF EXILIC EXAMPLES are woven not only through historical ac-
counts in scripture but also in the lives of those earnestly following Jesus
today. The person of exile may be considered a wanderer, a nomad, a
refugee, or a rebel. People of exile can be the marginalized, the disenfranchised, the outcast, the left out, and the pushed away. Different terms are
used, but separation defines them all. Exile is a dangerous and dominant
theme that runs through scripture, through the lives of the people of Israel, and through the universal church.

Graham Tomlin, in the foreword to Patrick Whitworth's book *Prepare
for Exile*, says, "Exile makes people re-evaluate what is important, adapt
to new conditions and rediscover their true identity, which can often get
blurred during periods of prosperity and ease."[1] Whitworth says, "Exile is
the church's best friend. This does not mean that it is easy or without suffering or hardship but if a review of church history has shown us anything
it is that exile has often been the price of change, renewal and at times
revival."[2] Gordon Mursell wrote in *Praying in Exile*: "The discovery that
exile is something all of us have to face, and out of the conviction that there
exist, for those willing to seek them out, priceless spiritual resources to help
us do so with hope and not despair."[3]

Alain Epp Weaver in his book *States of Exile*, writes (referring to John
Howard Yoder) that "Key to Yoder's understanding of exile is a particular

1. Tomlin, foreword to *Prepare for Exile*, vii.
2. Whitworth, *Prepare for Exile*, 97.
3. Mursell, *Praying in Exile*, 7.

reading of Scripture as the story of God's people responding to the call to depend on God alone."[4] Weaver goes on to say, "The exile thus represents, not a disruption in God's plans for his people, but rather an opportunity to return to radical dependence on God."[5] This is my understanding of the prophetic call of the people of God in general and the church in particular. How rare it is to find those who depend on God, much less depend on God alone for *everything*.

Women in Exile tells the stories of ten women who were exiled from their home countries for political and religious reasons. The author, Mahnaz Afkhami, exposes how various descriptions of inner exile are interconnected throughout their geographical and political exile. In describing these women, she says,

> They discovered the irreversible nature of their exile experience even when it became possible to return. They realized not only that their country had changed, but that they themselves are no longer who they were before they left. They learned that once one looks at one's home from the outside, as a stranger, the past, whether in the self or in the land, cannot be recaptured.[6]

Michael Frost says, "Exiles feel like a 'motherless child'—abandoned, rootless, vulnerable, orphaned."[7] He reminds us that "Jesus defines the first missionaries totally. His lifestyle, his passion, his teaching became the template for the actions of the first Christians. In the same way today, he should totally define those exiles seeking to follow him in a post-Christendom world."[8]

The role of exile is a key ingredient in the development of a new women's mission. It is seminal to the understanding of how a fresh hermeneutic can be explored in the realm of missiology. But as always, in order to forge the birthing of a new mission and possible movement, this mission must know the fire of conflict and exclusion.

4. Weaver, *States of Exile*, 27.
5. Ibid.
6. Afkhami, *Women in Exile*, 16.
7. Frost, *Exiles*, 9.
8. Ibid., 32.

A Multiplicity of Meaning

The myriad definitions of exile give a platform for discovering part of God's strategic ways. Exile is a significant ingredient in the lives of the women attracted to a women's mission. Most often the word exile has been understood as a geographical separation from one's home country. But the exilic component comes in different forms. Geographical, physical, political, emotional, spiritual, and ideological are all potential kinds of exile.

Karen Koehler quotes Michael Andre Bernstein as he shares his thoughts on exile:

> Whether it is a person, a stretch of shoreline, or the sound of a language, when something basic to one's identity has been torn away, nothing in the world is ever the same again . . . Exile is less like the death of one's beloved than like a betrayal from which it is impossible ever to become fully healed because the prospect of a pathway home, of a return that is almost a mutual pardoning, continues to exist. For the exile, hope is itself part of his (sic) torment.[9]

When discussing the different genres often associated with writing on the life of exile, Edward W. Said has this to say:

> Exile is strangely compelling to think about but terrible to experience. And while it is true that literature and history contain heroic, romantic, glorious even triumphant episodes in an exile's life, these are no more than efforts to overcome the crippling sorrow of estrangement. The achievements of exile are permanently undermined by the loss of something left behind forever.[10]

The impact of exile on an individual, a collective, or a movement is profound in its implications. The power of an exilic life is often energized by the embrace of the situation and is often a preparation for living and working in high-risk areas of the world. The willingness to embrace risk is strengthened because the person or person's worldview has been reconfigured. Without the embrace of exile the outcome will be one of bitterness and resentment, but with it comes the fruit of a life intent on pursuing God.

9. Koehler, "Angels of History," 257.

10. Said, *Reflections on Exile*, 173.

Definitions

Exile can be defined and ultimately understood in many ways. The weight of the word exile is broadened and brings a measure of understanding in the ways God uses or chooses separation for his followers. The voices in scripture that experienced this exile or separation in one form or another had a prophetic mandate to repeatedly bring the people of God into right alignment. Christian history is rife with examples of exile being one of God's ways to bring intimate formation to individuals and communities. Indeed, leverage was one of God's intentional ways to not only bring his people back from being ensnared by idol worship, but also to give those who had never heard an opportunity to walk in the ways of Yahweh.[11]

Exile is the experience of displacement. People who are exiled have been removed from their rightful place, from home, from country, from where they belong or long to be. There are different kinds of exile. There are exiles that result from political or social forces. Or one can suffer personal exile because of broken relationships and violations of trust. There is also religious exile, when a person has been displaced from his or her religious background or upbringing. One may have left or been forced out of the faith community that has been one's religious home, one's religious place. We can also speak of spiritual exile. This is not just removal from a religious tradition or the forsaking of a church. It is more. It is alienation from God, a profound feeling of abandonment by the Holy One. This spiritual exile can infect the other kinds of exile and deepen their already painful effects.[12]

Geographical exile can be described as being sent or choosing to go to another physical location, usually another country or continent. Often this is true of artists and writers, such as Ernest Hemingway, Gertrude Stein, Edna St. Vincent Millay, Dorothy Parker, and Pablo Picasso who moved to Paris in the 1920s and 1930s. In many ways they traveled to Europe in order to find out who they were as creative people, believing they could not find the truth without experiencing exile. This is certainly true of missionaries. Geographical exile is akin to physical exile, which has to do with movement within or without a setting or locality.

11. Theological understanding of the meaning of exile comes from a number of authors, including: Walter Brueggemann, *Prophetic Imagination, Hopeful Imagination, Cadences of Home*, and "Preaching to Exiles"; Erskine Clarke, *Exilic Preaching*; Stanley Hauerwas and William H. Willimon, *Resident Aliens*; Daniel L. Smith-Christopher, *Biblical Theology of Exile*; and Barbara Brown Taylor, *Leaving Church*.

12. Kelley, *Faith in Exile*, 21.

Both of these types of exile were instrumental in the lives of the desert monks and nuns in the fourth century. A monk named Gregory came to one of the Desert Fathers, and told him of a place he wanted to start a desert community. He jokingly said, "Everything that is not rock is ravine, everything that is not ravine is brambles, and all that are not brambles are overhanging cliffs. The path climbs up in overhang and is precipitous on all sides; it besets the spirit of the travelers and forces them into acrobatics for their own safety."[13] Basil the Great said it was "a worthy place of exile."[14] All who sought lives of exile in order to draw close to God did not demand the most desolate terrain, but many did.

"The desert fathers and mothers chose their barren locale because its values matched their own. They, too, opted to thrive on the boundary where life and death meet, living as simply as possible, with as few words as necessary, separated from the fragile anxieties of the world they had left behind."[15] Belden C. Lane goes on to explain: "Experiencing the terror of the desert under the controlled conditions of monastic life—being close to danger, but not too close—offered early Christian ascetics an ideal setting for reflecting on the sinner's relationship to a God of infinite majesty. The harsh landscape was interpreted within a *hermeneutical context* of fear tempered by grace."[16]

Political exile is often the most commonly understood definition: person or persons who have been sent or have chosen to leave their familiar dwelling or country because of political strife, difference of opinion, or oppression by a ruling or majority group in their country. Artists, poets, writers, activists who object to the government's agenda, beliefs, or activities were often sent into exile. "You will leave everything you love most: this is the arrow that the bow of exile shoots first. You will know how salty another's bread tastes and how hard it is to ascend and descend another's stairs"[17]

Some are exiled within their own country, like Aung San Suu Kyi in Burma. There are those who are "internally displaced people" in Burma, as well as in other countries. Political conflict, struggle, and violence within specific areas, disease, and so on, cause people to either become refugees

13. Gregory of Nazianzus, "Letter 4 to Basil," 19.

14. Lane, *Solace of Fierce Landscapes*, 161.

15. Ibid., 162.

16. Ibid., 164.

17. Dante, Paradise Canto 17:112.

on the borders or stay within their country and experience forced resettlement or worse, being constantly on the run through the jungles and on the mountains.

Emotional exile can be separation caused by trauma or heartbreak, relationship breakdown or withdrawal. An extreme form of this is mental exile, which can manifest itself or show itself through psychotic breaks or breakdowns. Often there is the element of grief and lament. Many who have experienced geographical exile also know intense emotional exile. The Israelites knew much about emotional exile. "By the rivers of Babylon we sat and wept when we remembered Zion" (Ps 137:1). The separation of friends or family due to calling, misunderstanding, or breach in trust can be a lingering lament that never leaves. Words from Zechariah express the anguish of emotional exile: "Wounded in the house of my friends" (Zech 13:6).

Spiritual exile can be more easily seen or felt when the presence of God seems to depart; when all that is known of God's love seems to be missing. As the book of Isaiah says, "The Lord has forsaken me, my Lord has forgotten me" (49:14). The believer can be awakened with both great yearning and passion for the Lord who seems to have left. Or the spiritual exile can bring bitterness of soul and a desolation that God does not intend. As Kelley said earlier, spiritual exile can affect all the other kinds of exile and make them even more painful.

Rabbi Jocee Hudson says, "To be in exile is a spiritual condition. We are in exile when we find ourselves somehow separated from God, separated from the sacred. We are in exile when we feel an absence of the divine in our lives. When we are in exile, we are spiritually marooned. Spiritually lost. Disconnected."[18] Whether the spiritual exile is real or imagined, the anguish gnaws unrelentingly. Some experience this dark night of exile, as living in-between two spheres, belief systems, borders, communities, or relationships. Marc Ellis says this concerning exile: "It is like being caught in a dream where words fall on deaf ears, and drift away into nothingness."[19]

"The word [exile] itself carries powerful connotations of sorrow and alienation, of the surrender of the individual to overwhelming strength, of years of fruitless waiting. There is also a lingering sense of defiance, a refusal to accept that what has happened can be permanent, an obsessive watch for any sign of weakness and decay in the enemy's camp which might

18. Hudson, "Parashat Sh'mot—Spiritual Exile."
19. Ellis, *Practicing Exile*, 29.

permit an eventual return. But what lasts the longest is the shock of the original expulsion."[20]

Descriptions

Isolation is an aspect within the area of exile. Isolation plays a large part in a person's development as the effects of exile shape it at certain junctures in her life. Shelley Trebesch says, "Some isolation experiences are deeper than others. St. John of the Cross uses the term 'Dark Night of the Soul' to describe an isolation experience in which God cannot be found. There is no felt presence of God. Some use the term 'Desert Experience' to show how dry the time can be."[21]

"The pain of the stripping process can be severe as God's sand paper removes the external identities. Even if leaders have entered a season of isolation by their own choice, the stripping process remains painful."[22] Embracing the exile, whether it is political, emotional, or otherwise, is the only way to grow through the process. For some the process takes a lifetime, because the goal is to know God. That is the reason for everything—to know God, to walk with Jesus, and to be led by the Holy Spirit.

Crucible events are often a major component of exile. These experiences have the potential to become catalytic in that they change not only individuals but the surrounding spheres of influence. For some, exile is the very crucible itself. For others, it is a lifelong "thorn in the flesh" that never finds resolution or healing. As Christians with the missional imperative, crucible moments can very well define decisions made not only for the rest of an individual's life, but for those they touch as well.

A crucible is a tipping point where new identities are weighed, where values are examined and strengthened or replaced, and where one's judgment and other abilities are honed. It is an incubator for new insights and a new conception of oneself. Often the transformational event in the crucible is a realization that one has power that affects other people's lives.[23]

Suffering is another component of exile. Suffering is not only fundamental to the understanding of exile but also to the understanding of the heart of God. We not only follow a missionary God, we follow a suffering

20. Simpson, *Oxford Book of Exile*, 1.
21. Trebesch, *Isolation*, 3.
22. Ibid., 37.
23. Bennis and Thomas, *Geeks and Geezers*, 106.

God. Many have embraced this understanding and have chosen to follow in the footsteps of Jesus; in so doing they have suffered in countless ways. Scripture speaks plainly of the suffering that is to be a signature of our way of life. Not only is it a hallmark, it is a promise that is given to all who choose to be his disciples.

Jesus said, "Blessed are you when people cast insults at you, and persecute you, and say all kinds of evil against you falsely, on account of me" (Matt 5:11). Not only are believers blessed when this happens, the response is not to be one of anger and resentment but one of loving kindness and humility. In the same chapter, Jesus says, "But I say to you, love your enemies and pray for those who persecute you" (Matt 5:44). Again Jesus reinforces this theme, "Remember the word that I said to you, 'A slave is not greater than his master.' If they persecuted me, they will also persecute you" (John 15:20). This again is a promise that Jesus gives to those who choose to follow him.

"Any biblical theology of mission must take suffering seriously," says Jude Tiersma-Watson in her chapter of the book, *Footprints of God*.[24] She states unequivocally that the issue of suffering is not often addressed among evangelical missiologists. But the world we live in today mandates that suffering be looked at with eyes that see the connection to the suffering of Jesus.

In studying the Old Testament, it is important to remember God's motivation for leading the Israelites into the desert to hunger and thirst. The suffering of the desert experience was intended to bring them into utter dependency and intimacy with God. From Jeremiah 2:2, we read: "Thus says the Lord, I remember the devotion of your youth, your love as a bride, how you followed me in the wilderness, in a land not sown." Hosea 2:14 (NASB) says, "Therefore, behold, I will allure her, bring her into the wilderness and speak kindly to her (upon her heart)." The Israelites were looking for authentic faith. This wildness of God's love and the rawness of God's mercy can ultimately be found in the desert. This is the redemptive reason for suffering—unending friendship with our God! It is actually a gift from God. Mother Teresa often made this plain as she would pick up the destitute and dying and hold them in her arms during their last moments. The nature of exile brings suffering into focus. The words of scripture are clear: "For you have been called for this purpose, since Christ suffered for you, leaving you an example for you to follow in his steps" (1 Pet 2:21).

24. Tiersma-Watson, "Mother Teresa," 121.

No matter what kind of exile is experienced, it is a vital ingredient in shaping the heart of a woman called to minister in high-risk areas. How she chooses to die to herself in the midst of isolation and exile, will often determine how God will use her in the future. Exile can become a sacred place ordained to bring one closer to God.

FOUR

Outside the Camp

WOMEN OFTEN FIND THEMSELVES excluded from leadership positions, trailblazing opportunities, and pioneering situations, as well as being barred from strategic planning. These exclusions in part define an outsider perspective. This chapter explores the ways in which outsider thinking can be an asset to one's walk with God in pioneering work.

First, scriptural directives are considered in order to see what God says about the notion of being outside the camp. Secondly, the outsider explication is looked at from two angles: (1) Christian women missionaries who are denied access to decision making; and (2) women outside the church. These are unpacked as social movement theory is brought into play. An outsider interpretation is critical in order to recognize the call for a new mission.

Scriptural Insight

My objective here is not to do an intensive study of God's view of the poor and the marginalized but to look briefly at some of Jesus's teaching. Turning to scripture we find God's intentionality. The insiders were usually found in the temple preaching the Law. They were the traditionalists that were comfortable in their setting and in their belief system. When Jesus came on the scene, he spoke directly to the Pharisees, the Sadducees, and the common people.

In the Gospel of Matthew, Jesus said repeatedly when referring to the Law, to the ancients, to Torah, "You have heard that it was said . . . but I say to you . . . " (Matt 5:21–22, 27–28, 31–32, 33–34, 38–39, 43–44). In one short chapter, Jesus consistently shows how the Law was but a shadow. The authority with which he spoke stunned the people. He countered their traditions and they were amazed at his teaching. Jesus was concerned with the weightier issues of justice, mercy, and faith (Matt 23:23). When Jesus cleared the temple, preached the Sermon on the Mount, and reached out to women like Mary Magdalene, the Pharisees' anger rose up because the "insider message" was being corrupted. The Law-keepers were livid. The rich man walked away in sadness when he realized he must come to God naked and alone. Jesus kept telling the people where they could find him, and it was "outside the camp" not inside the temple.

> Therefore Jesus also suffered outside the city gate in order to sanc-tify the people by his own blood. Let us then go to him outside the camp and bear the abuse he endured. For here we have no lasting city, but we are looking for the city that is to come. (Heb 13:12–14)

Being outside the camp was a lonely place, a despised place. It was full of shame and humiliation and scandal. Jesus was all those things and more. He became sin for us; Jesus was crucified outside the city gate, and in many ways he calls us to embrace the abuse that he suffered. The scandal of the Cross became the hallmark of the early Christians.

In Frank Anthony Spina's book *The Faith of the Outsider*, he tells the stories of seven people who were outsiders in scripture, including the women Rahab, Ruth, and the woman at the well. Two women are found in the Old Testament, but in addition, he goes on to give examples from the New Testament.

Nevertheless, to say that the New Testament has its own version of the outsider motif does not go far enough, for the very essence of New Testa-ment thought is rooted in the conviction that God's designs for Israel have come to fruition in what God did in and through Jesus, Israel's Messiah/Christ. Thus, the outsider theme is not incidental in the New Testament but at the core of its central message.[1]

Spina says, "It turns out that this business of insiders and outsiders is a complex theological matter."[2] He makes the point by using the story of Naa-man and Gehazi to show that there are different levels of being an outsider. He says, referring to Naaman, "that he is not only an outsider but an enemy

---

1. Spina, *Faith of the Outsider*, 137.
2. Ibid., 73.

outsider."[3] He goes on to talk about Naaman being a "highly accomplished outsider" and a "prominent outsider." When discussing Naaman's leprosy, Spina says, "The main issue having to do with Naaman's ailment is religious and theological, not clinical. The most serious consequence of being afflicted with this malady was being cut off from God's people and, more particularly, not having access to the temple for worship."[4] Naaman was not an Israelite, but a true outsider, even an enemy outsider!

That Naaman chose to go to the Jordan River hoping to be healed made his status as an outsider even more suspect. One would think that Naaman's deep gratitude to the God of Israel for healing his leprosy would bring inclusion with the people of God, but it was not to be. The last thing that Elisha said to him was "Go in peace" (2 Kgs 5:19). Naaman remained an outsider in the eyes of the Israelite world but not in the eyes of God. This is important to understand because women coming to Christ from very far outside the camp and then joining together will probably still be outsiders in the eyes of the church, but most definitely not in the eyes of the eternal God.

An Outsider Interpretation

Movements are built by people from the edges, those who have been relegated to an outsider status. They are people that could be called outcasts, refugees, pilgrims, and foreigners—those who long for something more as they are attempting to rise up out of the brokenness of their own lives. They come from different classes and socio-economic strata. Some are nomads and some wanderers, if not geographically, then certainly emotionally and spiritually. They know a set-apartness that is not necessarily chosen; it has been forced upon them. Whatever status or label they have been given; these are the people that build grassroots organizations, communities, and movements.

In the introduction to his book *The Dynamics of Christian Mission*, Paul E. Pierson says,

> Mission movements always appear to have risen on the periphery of the broader church. Those who have responded to the missionary call have always been a minority, often perceived with disdain or rejection by their societies and even their churches. Yet, they

3. Ibid., 74.
4. Ibid., 77.

persevered, and despite their apparent failures, God "did exceed-
ingly abundantly" above all they had hoped. Often, like their Lord,
these missionaries were grains of wheat that fell into the ground
and died in order that fruit would come later.[5]

The marginalized going to the marginalized in order to bring suste-
nance, this is the essence of an outsider hermeneutic that can be applied to
mission work. It is the "outside the camp" scenario that Jesus talked about
and lived. He was regularly ministering to those who were the outsiders
and those who were oppressed, those who were known sinners and those
who were despised. Jesus is now on the highways and byways waiting for
his friends and followers to join him with those in prison, those who are
poor, those who are scorned, those who have no home, and those who have
been forced into exile.

Orlando E. Costas makes the following statement in *Christ Outside
the Gate:*

> Jesus died outside the gate, and in so doing changed the place of
> salvation and clarified the meaning of mission. No longer can I see
> God's grace as an individual benefit, a privileged possession or a
> religious whitewash that enables me to feel good and continue to
> live the old way because my bad conscience has been soothed and
> my guilt feelings washed away. On the contrary, because salvation
> is to be found in the crucified Son of God who died outside the
> gate of the religious compound, to be saved by faith in him is to
> experience transformation that makes me a "debtor" to the world
> (Rom 1:14) and calls me forth to share in his suffering by serving,
> especially the lowest representatives: the poor, the powerless and
> the oppressed.[6]

Individuals living on the edge form movements; forge them into communities through the fires of discontent. When a group of people, a community, or a true movement gathers steam it will of necessity be at odds
with the existing authority structure, the powers. There will be tension,
struggle, and controversy, which is why new communities and organizations are often called prophetic, whether they are within the body of Christ
or not. To walk in the prophetic is to walk the road of struggling for justice
on behalf of those who are lacking. To gain a more comprehensive perspective, it is good to look at the understanding of movements in general as

5. P. Pierson, *Dynamics of Christian Mission*, 5.
6. Costas, *Christ Outside the Gate*, 194.

they have grown from disenfranchised people coming together and forming community.

Consensus and Conflict Movements

The choice to compare "consensus movements" and "conflict movements" is helpful in understanding the outsider perspective. *Frontiers in Social Movement Theory* is a compilation of articles written by different authors that specifically deals with these two types of movements.[7] They are shown as two opposite views when applying social movement theory. One is that "consensus movements" can foster substantial and lasting change by working through the system. Michael Schwartz and Shuva Paul, in their article "Resource Mobilization versus the Mobilization of People," state that "consensus movements may be seen as an outgrowth of what has been called the 'bureaucratization of social discontent.'"[8] They believe that consensus movements have very little long-term effect on social change. "This is a basic contradiction in consensus groups: their strength—broad institutional support—becomes their weakness."[9]

Conflict movements on the other hand, challenge existing models and motifs of established organizations and ways of thinking. Ultimately, the conflict movement demands change by confronting the prevailing power structure; in this case, the traditional missionary structure would be challenged.[10]

In due course, it seems that both approaches are part of a continuum and both have constraints. Both can be applied to the emergence of a unique women's mission, which could become a forerunner for a new movement. While some women may be better suited to bring about change from the inside, it must be the outsider that initiates the change. In the end, it comes down to commitment and strategy. Belief that a great need must be met and the commitment to band together no matter what the outcome are vital for a community to grow into a movement as it gains momentum.

We are confronted with the insider understanding that established missionary organizations must adhere to a traditional belief system that believes women should not be in positions of top leadership, and also that

7. Morris and Mueller, *Frontiers in Social Movement Theory*.
8. Schwartz and Paul, "Resource Mobilization," 205.
9. Ibid., 215.
10. Ibid., 204–23.

women should not be sent into high-risk areas. They consider it best to work through the system and slowly change the minds of those in control.

The outsider approach believes that for any type of social change to happen, whether inside or outside the church, there must be a separate conflict movement that rises up to make historic change for the good of the church in the long run. This could very well be a prophetic statement that is lived out in the lives of the women who decide to embrace the call to be misunderstood but who hold strongly to the belief that in the end more good will come.

God often speaks through the outsider in order to call attention to needs and attitudes that require action. Most often these have to do with justice issues not being met, the poor not being cared for, and the marginalized not being brought into the fold. I would posit that this is the true nature of God's prophetic people. For some, the prophetic life bears the unmistakable imprint of God's longing. For others, God uses prophetic people to bring specific words. For a new women's mission, we would primarily embrace the prophetic as a lifestyle that calls for others to return to the mandate of Jesus.

Stephen B. Bevans and Roger P. Schroeder have written a book called *Prophetic Dialogue*. They clearly remind us, quoting Paul VI, that "the Holy Spirit is the principal agent of evangelization." They go on to say, "In a real way the history of mission is the history of the Holy Spirit, the history of God 'inside out' in creation. Our great privilege and grace as church is to somehow be participants, sacraments actually, of that history of love, healing, liberation and prophetic dialogue."[11]

A Fresh Way of Seeing

Theories of interpretation are necessary if one is going to understand the context in which one finds oneself. Creating hermeneutical openings or space is essential for those who desire to lead with inspiration and grounded vision. As stated earlier, I am using "hermeneutic" in the sense of having a new or fresh interpretation, a deeper understanding. Gadamer defines "the task of hermeneutics as the bridging of personal or historical distance between the minds."[12]

11. Bevans and Schroeder, *Prophetic Dialogue*, 137.
12. Gadamer, *Philosophical Hermeneutics*, 181.

In the context of this book, it is the bridging of the minds that I find most compelling. It lessens the distance between what the traditional missionary community understands about women on the frontlines of ministry and what could actually be happening. Filling in these gaps of understanding is critical if change is to be forthcoming. To say it another way, it is important that the breach between the old missionary way of life with its strict candidate procedures and protocols be bridged into a fresh wind of the Spirit characterized by a new women's mission where new qualifications, requirements, and the reality of grace are put into place. The familiar must make way for a new expression of kingdom activity in the postmodern age. Resistance to a new move is unfortunately to be expected, but it is in the refining fire of conflict that a prophetic community is birthed. The struggle to see beyond the seen is not only imperative for those women who have been pushed aside but it is essential for a walk of faith.

The case for a fresh hermeneutic has been developed as a strategy for change. It is important to understand the underpinnings and to answer the questions of bridge-building if the foundation is to be firm. Looking at possible components of this new model brings in the discussion of power as seen through the eyes of one who views situations, ideas, and belief systems from the outside. For my purposes here this is called an "outsider hermeneutic."

This idea of an "outsider hermeneutic" is a return to the way that Jesus engaged his band of followers. As outsiders themselves, Jesus showed them the way to minister to the marginalized who were also outsiders. This is what was done in the beginning and now, in the twenty-first century, this is what is required. This outside hermeneutic is the heart of God with a fresh application for today.

One example of adjusting the way in which we see ideas, challenges, or the people around us is to consider what Elaine Heath calls the "hermeneutic of love."[13] In many ways, she restates the motivation of Mother Teresa of Calcutta, Jackie Pullinger of Hong Kong, and Heidi Baker of Mozambique, whose ministries are driven both by love; first, love for Jesus, and second, as real love of others by focusing on the One person that is in front of them.[14] Heath says, "The hermeneutic of love is grounded in the belief that Jesus really does live in people around us, that Jesus thirsts in our actual neigh-

---

13. Heath, *Mystic Way of Evangelism*, 119.

14. See Mother Teresa and Kolodiejchuk, *Come Be My Light* and H. Baker and R. Baker, *Always Enough*.

bors. Jesus is bound with eternal love to every person I encounter. This is the starting point." She goes on to say, "With a hermeneutic of love I give myself in prayer and friendship to the people around me, not so that I can get something from them, not even a commitment to join my church, but so that I can minister to Jesus in them, Jesus who thirsts."[15]

The theory of a hermeneutic of love is grounded on scriptural principles and the words of Jesus: "Truly I tell you, just as you did not do it to one of the least of these, you did not do it to me" (Matt 25:45). Heath retells the story of a woman who was not welcome anywhere; she was the woman who had been hemorrhaging for twelve years and because of the bleeding she was considered unclean. She was not wanted. She lived the life of an outsider who had been forced into exile by her own community. But Heath points out that Jesus looked at her in a different way from those who were around her. He looked at her with great love and touched her with deep healing.

Communities have forced many into exile for reasons not filled with grace. Not being willing to identify with another's burden or pain or sin has brought a profound wounding that never seems to heal. Heath says, "How can any of us know why another person falls? We are a complex mixture of wounds and needs and sin."[16]

Living out this hermeneutic of love is often focused primarily on those who have not yet come to Christ. But I would assert that a new way of seeing with eyes of love must be worked out in the church at large and the missionary world in particular. To do this, there are a plethora of women on the mission field who have also felt forsaken and left out of ministry service because of gender bias and old ways of looking at missions. The agony of exile could be eased by embracing this fresh way of looking at the missional mandate of believers.

In summary, as always, we are pointed to the Cross. In our weakness, God's grace is sufficient. David Bosch, in his small and powerful book *A Spirituality of the Road*, remembers a conversation with Kosuke Koyama.

> He compares the hands of the Crucified with those of Lenin and of the Buddha. If Jesus' hands were closed tight like that of Lenin's, theology would become ideology. If his [Jesus] hands were open, very much open, with symbolic webs between the fingers so as to be able to scoop up everybody, like the hands of the Buddha,

15. Heath, *Mystic Way of Evangelism*, 125.
16. Ibid., 130.

theology would lose its quality of being a stumbling-block. But now his hands are neither open, nor closed; they are defenseless and pierced through.[17]

It is enough to say that it is a privilege to go outside the city gate, to live outside the camp. To dwell with those whom the world or church deems unworthy is a great joy. This is the place where Jesus says we will find the very presence of God for that is where he will be found.

17. D. Bosch, *Spirituality of the Road*, 81.

PART III

Pioneering Women Missionaries

I am your message, Lord.

Throw me like a blazing torch into the night,

that all may see and understand what it means to be a disciple.

SAINT MARIA SKOBTSOVA,
ORTHODOX NUN AND MARTYR (1891–1945)

FIVE

Historical Undergirding

TWO HISTORICAL PIECES OR time periods are examined in this chapter. First we explore the historical background of asceticism, which involves the practice of self-denial and focus on the fruit of the Spirit. Often, the person's life was spent living in austerity and longing for deeper intimacy with God. Second, the monastic life, which emerged from the early church, as a few people longed for an authentic faith with God; a faith not mired in the trappings of the institutional. The fourth-century monastic ways help to unravel the early years of the Desert Mothers as they began to carve out a way of life in exile and in essence became an exilic community. We take an excursion into the desert life of the monastic. Three women are showcased, highlighting a prophetic lifestyle and showing the call of repentance through exile and ultimately friendship.

Next we leap to the nineteenth century and investigate the women who were not only fighting for the right to vote but also fighting for the right to go to the ends of the earth in order to preach the gospel. Lastly, an exilic theology with various scripture references is discussed as a potent response to the power of conversion.

Desert Movement: Fourth Century

My task here is to make a case for the consideration of a lifestyle no longer seen as valid or appropriate for the time in which we live. In order to do that we must go back to the fourth century and look at the beginnings of what

I see as the first women's movement. It just so happens that it was birthed in the desert.

Much of the Protestant part of the body of Christ is undernourished when it comes to the feast that could be theirs in the realm of desert theology, also known as exilic theology, and in particular the Desert Mothers of old. Not enough has been written but what has found its way from pen to paper, from paper to computer is often hastily scanned and then quickly discarded because of the tendency on behalf of Protestants to think that this particular brand of theology doesn't have it quite right.

A major reason for very little information on the women monastics/nuns is that those who were writing the history of monasticism and the Desert Fathers did so believing that the women of the desert were not as significant as their male counterparts.[1] Shortly after she became an Episcopal priest, Mary C. Earle began to wonder where all the women were. She writes, "I would walk around, asking out loud, 'Where are my mothers?' 'Where are my sisters?'"[2] I too asked similar questions after I became a believer. I wondered where the women preachers, evangelists, leaders, and teachers could be found. Where were the women? Who could I learn from? Later, I wondered where all the information and writing about the women who fled to the desert in the early days of the monastic tradition could be found.

"Early church histories frequently made mention of women living in the desert, living as urban solitaries or residing in or near monastic communities. Palladius, in his Lausiac history, estimated that the women outnumbered the men two to one, yet it is the stories of the men that are preserved and told."[3] Misogyny was rife and only recently have female scholars begun to unearth the lives of these remarkable women who have been passed over. Earle has this to say:

> Thanks to women scholars of the last generation, we are discovering that the women were there all along. We are discovering, often through painstaking, detailed examination of primary texts (scraps of papyrus, fragments of vellum, hints and illusions in texts written by men) that women played an essential role in the early years of the Christian faith. . . . They were seeking to live out the faith in Christ crucified, resurrected, and living in ways that were

1. Forman, *Praying with the Desert Mothers*, 1–2.
2. Earle, *Desert Mothers*, 1.
3. Swan, *Forgotten Desert Mothers*, 3.

authentic and true to the gospel. They were spiritual guides. They were teachers. They were leaders of their monastic communities. And some of them, as Christianity became an official religion of the Roman Empire, became what are known as the "desert mothers" or "*ammas.*"[4]

Historical Background

The early church was primarily a house-church movement in a home-faith environment. Women had begun to hold positions of leadership as deacons, elders, and presbyters, as the Jesus movement was clearly a way of equality for women in the early church. As women chose to follow Jesus in the movement called "the Way," sometimes referred to as choosing the "Way of Life," their lives were given greater meaning. Women were involved in teaching, preaching, evangelism, and laboring to bring God's love to the poor. Women were accepted as prophets, healers, and ascetics, although the prophetic role of women was often found outside the church. "It was much easier for bishops to monitor and influence teachers than they could those who claimed to be prophets speaking in the name of the Lord."[5]

There were many dynamics of the time that contributed to the intensification of monastic lifestyles. Chief among them was what could be called the "Constantinian captivity." Being a Christian had lost the radical, prophetic mandate that it once had. Christianity had become acceptable and no longer was there a cost involved. In a short amount of time, the church had gone from being very much "outside the camp," marginalized, persecuted, and martyred, to the gaining of respect and legislating "Christianized" laws through the nominal at best Christian emperor Constantine in the fourth century.[6] Shenk has this to say: "Whenever the church is controlled by culture, it forfeits its prophetic word."[7] This is precisely what happened when Constantine legalized Christianity; the church became domesticated, tamed, and controlled. No longer was it the fervent abandonment that the early believers had lived.

4. Earle, *Desert Mothers*, 1–2.

5. Swan, *Forgotten Desert Mothers*, 7.

6. Malone, *Women and Christianity*, 133. For more insight during the reign of Constantine see Malone, *Women and Christianity*; Chryssaygis, *Heart of the Desert*; Harmless, *Desert Christian*; and Swan, *Forgotten Desert Mothers*.

7. Shenk, *Write the Vision*, 7.

The early disciples turned the world upside down. "Since the days of Paul in the New Testament, Christians who brought the message of Jesus Christ have been charged with interfering with the established order."[8] But now there was no longer a counter-cultural mentality among many Christians. They decided to settle into normal society and make a life for themselves. Christendom took over the church and in so doing, left no alternative for those seeking to radically follow God. The church had been tamed by the world! Shenk makes this comment: "The way to regain integrity is to return to the evangelizing task. This will require that we break free from the Christendom mentality, on the one hand, and captivity to culture on the other, for that kind of church has effectively been neutered."[9]

The odor of institutionalized Christianity became a stench in the nose of those who longed for something more. There was no longer a prophetic edge among the followers of Christ. Due to secularization, cultural mainstreaming, and other factors, a growing dissatisfaction among believers began to take shape. Out of the dust of pomp and protocol in Constantine's court came a deep longing for the reality of the living God, a passionate ache to encounter the presence of God. The hunger for holiness in the midst of a culture of compromise drove women and men into the desert.

Elizabeth A. Clark makes the statement, "The demise of martyrdom as a way to manifest one's Christian commitment and the increased numbers of less-than-ardent Christians within the fourth century church are often given as reasons for the popularity of asceticism in this period."[10] Women especially were fed up with mainstream Christendom because they had experienced relative equality in the early church and a freedom they had never known. But now male dominance was asserting itself in the church just as it was in society. It is no wonder that women chose to go into small wilderness communities of other likeminded women or else live solitary lives in the desert.

"After a generation or two of desert living, the limits of living the ascetic life in such conditions were recognized, and the ascetics developed into yet another form to facilitate their goals. The name given this form is monasticism."[11] Patricia Ranft writes with scholarly understanding and brings to light the hidden treasure of this time period. Not all women left

8. Robert, *Christian Mission*, 88.

9. Shenk, *Write the Vision*, 75.

10. Clark, *Women in the Early Church*, 115.

11. Ranft, *Women and Spiritual Equality*, 57.

the desert life but many chose to develop likeminded communities, monastic in nature. A woman's right to choose was birthed in the early years. The right to choose became the way to escape the confines of marriage and societal restriction, and run with abandon to the desert to be exiled with Christ, her Beloved. "[This] was the period in which Christian women came into their own as models of the pious life and as mentors for others, setting examples of devout living that could be imitated by the next generations of females."[12]

Diana Butler Bass says in *A People's History of Christianity*, "'Come follow me' became a literal practice of devotion, an act of leaving behind the known world for the unknown journey to God."[13] "For those who went to the desert 'come follow me' was not an escape; rather it served as an alternative practice of engagement—the first step on the way to becoming a new people."[14]

"Experiencing the terror of the desert under the controlled conditions of monastic life—being close to danger, but not too close—offered early Christian ascetics an ideal setting for reflecting on the sinner's relationship to a God of infinite majesty. The harsh landscape was interpreted within a hermeneutical context of fear tempered by grace."[15] Belden C. Lane goes on to say, "The desert has to lead us, at last, from aloneness with God (in a moment of great and silent emptiness) to community with others, from the loss of the fragile self to the discovery of a new identity binding us to the world."[16]

Whatever the reason for women first going to the desert to live in exile and then their vocations evolving into monastic communities, it became clear that monasticism would change the face of Christianity and be used by God as a tool for missionary advancement throughout the world. The term monastic-missionary community takes on deeper meaning. From the seeds of discontent and hunger for God grew a movement energized by the mercy of God.

---

12. Clark, *Women in the Early Church*, 19.

13. Bass, *People's History of Christianity*, 46.

14. Ibid., 48.

15. Lane, *Solace of Fierce Landscapes*, 164.

16. Ibid., 232.

Desert Asceticism

As a response to the call of God to live in exile, the ascetic found her way to the barren desert. Benedicta Ward makes this comment in her book *Harlots of the Desert*: "The way (for women) to have a place in the world of early monasticism, was to transcend gender differences whether by life in a single sex community, or by undertaking a solitary form of life in which it was more prudent, for example in the desert where there were hostile marauders, for a woman to dress as a man." She goes on to say, "Life in the desert, *anachoreisis*, was a practical demonstration of freedom from the limitations and responsibilities of society."[17] Women who chose the desert life of exile did so for many reasons, but the chief goal was to find union with God.

Later, monasteries and nunneries began to dot the landscape. (The term monastic and monastery were used by female nuns and monks as well.) As these communities grew, there was the natural progression to the outer edge by more radical women (and men). The Holy Spirit was calling them to the desert life of exile. This desert tradition of intense fasting and prayer attracted many women as they sought true intimacy with God. In a profound sense, the women following God into the desert became the first "women's movement" and, as mentioned earlier, some scholars believe that there were more women than men living in communities or alone in the desert. Their heart's desire was freedom to be wholly given to God.

The Desert Mothers or spiritual mothers, or *ammas* as they were called, lived an ascetic lifestyle to which others were often drawn. Some of the *ammas* were connected to homes, some formed monasteries, and others went out alone into the desert. Often, younger women would follow them and become disciples, and then another community would form. Communities grew as the vocational call was answered. Abandoned buildings, ruins, and caves were common places to live, but these communities of women could also be found a day's walk from a town or gathered around a church. Going far out in the desert would usually be seen as a woman's decision to put to death the flesh and do battle with the demonic. The more forsaken the place: the more intense the battle within and without.

The "cell" became the center of a woman's life; the place where she did spiritual battle against her own inner desires and struggles. Laura Swan describes the cell in this way: "A simple course mat, a sheepskin, a lamp,

17. Ward, *Harlots of the Desert*, 62–63.

and vessels for water and oil were the common contents of the ascetic's home. Usually the ascetic would eat one simple, often vegetarian meal a day. Sleep was kept to a minimum, both as an ascetical practice and to leave more time for prayer."[18]

Doing penance for one's sins was indeed common, but this is not the whole truth. The crying out for mercy, such as doing penance, was often a response in gratitude to God for the already great gift of grace which had been given to them. It was also a prophetic statement that modeled repentance for those who did not yet know Christ.

I would argue that a desert/exilic theology of mercy goes to the heart of the response of conversion to Christ and produces a radicalized/prophetic lifestyle. The power of conversion goes beyond the boundaries of common church life, in that radical sinners have great potential to make radical disciples of Jesus Christ. It is in the realm of exile that a theology of the desert can clearly be seen, notably in the lives of notorious sinners who became anchorites, who then grew into *ammas*. In reality, the prophetic nature of the call to exile is profound.

Women of Prophetic Promise

Since the aim of the ascetics or Desert Mothers was simply to disappear into exile and find union with God, there has not been much to extract in terms of stories and sayings. And yet, there are a few fragments that remain. It is to this that we turn.

There were many women of the desert who were so notorious in their former sins that in their turning became infamous for their piety and intimacy with God. Once they were known as prostitutes, but soon they became known as desert lovers of God. Their very choices brought forth a prophetic lifestyle. Not so much with the words they spoke but with the lives they lived, were they able to exhibit the passionate heart of God in ways that put to shame the common "pew sitter" of the day.[19]

Such was Pelagia, a woman who lived in Antioch and then later near Jerusalem. It is thought that she lived during the time of Emperor Numerianus (283–284). But the dates are sketchy, though it is certain she did live

---

18. Swan, *Forgotten Desert Mothers*, 11.
19. Ward, *Harlots of the Desert*.

before 407, "because St. John Chrysostom (c. 347–407) used the example of her life in one of his homilies to encourage sinners not to despair."[20]

An actress and a prostitute for many years, Pelagia came to the Lord through the preaching of a monk-bishop named Nonnos. One day, when her carriage was passing by, he saw her and began to cry so intensely that his clothes were soaked in tears. He went to his home and prayed all night for her, asking God to forgive him for not being as diligent in pursuing Christ as this woman was in pursuing her lovers.[21]

The next day, she was compelled to go to the town church where she heard Nonnos preach the gospel. She sent a letter to him saying, "I have heard O saint of God, from a certain Christian, that the Master came not 'to call the righteous, but sinners to repentance'; that He does not despise even loathsome harlots, thieves and tax collectors. Much rather, He, whom the Cherubim dare not gaze upon, associated and conversed with them."[22] She begged him to let her come and repent of all her sins, which she did. She was baptized and then gave all her possessions, clothes, jewelry, and money to the poor, the widows, and the orphans. In giving everything away, she said, "For me the ultimate wealth is my Bridegroom, the Master Christ."[23]

Not long after this, Pelagia left Antioch and went to Jerusalem under cover of night. She lived in exile as a hermit and fought the demons of her past as the enemy of her soul tried to lure her back into sin. But she chose to spend the rest of her life in a cave near Jerusalem. No one knew until her death that the supposed monk, Father Pelagios, who gave such wise counsel, was really a woman, as she dressed in men's clothes.

Saint Pelagia the Penitent received much mercy and at the heart of her repentance was a longing to be close to the only Lover who would ever know the depths of her heart. She remains a prophetic witness in that her life shows how far God will go to redeem the sinner and speak forgiveness to all those who will come to Him. Again, exile was used to bring intimacy.[24]

Evodikia of Heliopolis in Phoenicia, born during the horrific reign of Trajan (98–117), was another infamous woman who became a lover of God in the desert. Having grown wealthy from selling herself to men, she was quite comfortable in her surroundings. She lived next door to a house

20. *Lives of the Spiritual Mothers*, 457.
21. Ibid., 463.
22. Ibid., 460.
23. Ibid., 463.
24. *Lives of the Spiritual Mothers*, 456–66.

that Father Germanos had come to visit. He began to preach about the last judgment and the condemnation of sinners. He preached so loudly that she heard him through the walls of her house and began to sob at the conviction of the Holy Spirit. She was filled with fear and sent her servant next door to ask him to come and tell her what she must do to be saved! At first she thought she must only repent of her great wealth gotten through illicit means, but he explained that it was through her sinful acts that the riches were obtained. Evdokia went on to give away all she owned to the needy and afflicted, the poor, the widows, and the orphans. She left her past life far behind to welcome exile and proceeded to join a community of sisters, taking vows and embracing the monastic life.[25]

Paesia was also a woman who lived in Egypt in the fourth century. She became a recluse in the desert after a life of sexual favors and consequent shame. In order to bring her out of the lifestyle she had chosen, God sent a monk to her and he said, "What have you got against Jesus that you behave like this?"[26] As he started to cry, the conviction became overwhelming and she began to sob. The gift of repentance was given in those moments. From that day forward she went off into the desert of Scete and lived there, sleeping on the sand, longing for the lover of her soul, Christ Jesus.

There were many others who had pursued a life full of pleasure, indulgence, and self-absorption. When they came to the end of themselves, often through the preaching of the Word, their lives were turned upside down. Many of the desert dwellers drawn to exile had gifts of healing, discernment, wisdom, words of knowledge, and the multiplying of food, along with other numerous miracles. They chose an intensity of life in running after their Beloved, which allowed God to trust them with signs and wonders for the benefit of the poor and needy who would seek them out in the exile of the desert in order to enquire of their wisdom.[27]

The lives of these women and those who followed after them are examples of their courage, as well as their weakness. The stigma of finding Jesus in the desert was present because the women gave all to find and touch the mystery of our Triune God. Their resolve to proclaim that Jesus alone is God brought disdain, ridicule, and contempt. Many of them paid the price through martyrdom.

---

25. Ibid., 92–114.

26. Swan, *Forgotten Desert Mothers*, 96.

27. Ward, *Harlots of the Desert*.

The Sacred Place of Exile

Theology in the Desert

Desert theology has many detractors, but the emphasis on suffering should not be overlooked. Those who chose to establish their way of life in the desert were not looking for the assurance of salvation. This understanding of God was not of salvific significance but of sanctification and intimate tenderness of relationship with the Savior. It does not mean that the work on the cross was insufficient, or that anything must be added to obtain redemption. Nevertheless, there is room for discussion concerning the place of suffering in the life of the believer, in this case the early monastic believer. It is my contention that working out one's salvation in fear and trembling finds a significant place in the lives of those living in exile.

Specific texts are foundational for understanding the heart of the desert lovers of God. The book of Song of Songs, which Solomon is thought to have written, is one of these. In the early church it was widely believed to be an allegory of love from Christ the Beloved to the church, both corporately and individually. The early Christians followed in the same vein of belief as their Jewish counterparts, believing it was a book celebrating the love of God for Israel.

Apponius (c. 500), a hidden monk who was not well known, wrote a commentary on the Song of Songs, most of which, except for a few excerpts, has not yet been published. He and others wrestled with God in their monasteries and desert lives in order to comprehend the ways of the Beloved. Apponius said,

> It is not enough that the filth of our sins has been washed away in baptism or that our soul receives the kisses of Christ . . . or that she has been introduced into the storeroom of knowledge of the divine Scripture; or that she preserves unchanged the straight path of the faith as the apostles handed it down—it is not enough, unless she put behind her the good things she has done, and with all her strength, stretch herself out ahead, by seeking, by searching and by knocking—toward that which has not yet been attained.[28]

These words are used to engender a compelling in the heart of the new penitent. In comparison to all the loves she has known, she cries out, "Your love is better." It is for the love of God that she makes the choice of exile and hides herself in the desert wrapped in the presence of the Beloved. The manifold affections of God draw the individual to run after Jesus on

28. Norris, *Song of Songs*, 52.

54

the mountaintops and into the desert. "Draw me after You and let us run together" (Song 1:4). This book is on the short list for foundational exilic theology often found in the desert.

The book of Hosea is easily understood as a model for understanding God's heart toward the wandering lust-filled life of Israel and also for the individual needing restoration. "Therefore, behold, I will allure her, bring her into the wilderness and speak kindly to her" (3:14). Here we have the desert being shown as a place not only of repentance and restoration but also of intimacy. Again, we see the choice of exile.

Jesus spoke the words: "Unless a grain of wheat fall into the earth and dies, it remains by itself alone, but if it dies, it bears much fruit" (John 12:24). The women called to a life of exile wholly believed that true life was found only in death to self. The most radical response to God for being forgiven much is to love much (Luke 7:47). It is God who must be loved first. To be passionately united with him was the deepest longing of their hearts in gratitude for his great mercy in forgiving their sins. When Jesus said those words, he saw not only Mary Magdalene's heart, but also those who would follow after her throughout history. There would be many who would come to the foot of the Cross and pour out the best of their lives for the sake of his love. Giving all they had, the Desert Mothers in return were given all they needed in Jesus himself.

The following text is shrouded in mystery, and yet the lovers of the desert took these words seriously and chose to live their lives accordingly. The early church was often fond of quoting this scripture:

> Now I rejoice in my sufferings for your sake, and in my flesh I do
> my share on behalf of His body (which is the church) in filling up
> that which is lacking in Christ's afflictions. (Col 1:24)

The suffering embraced in the desert was no small thing. Turning their backs on the world was a visceral response to the darkness of their own hearts.

Another aspect of desert theology is repentance through friendship—the ever alluring and sought after friendship with God. It was the only requirement that could satisfy the hunger of the soul. James 4:4 says, "Friendship with the world is hostility toward God." Their greatest desire was to know friendship with God and so they denied themselves, left the world behind, and took up the mantle of suffering as did the prophets of old. For years these women had passionately pursued any relationship that could be found. But it was the kindness of God that brought them to repentance so that relationship with the Triune God could be found. True intimacy can be found in exile.

These radicalized women chose not to stay within what had become a normative, lukewarm, and indifferent belief system that denied the reality of God. Wild women of the early centuries knew what they had been saved from and longed to gaze into the face of Jesus alone. The Holy Spirit has drawn them and the power of deep conversion compelled them to embrace exile. The radical sinner became a radical lover of God. The women of exile who were redeemed from sin, highlights the goal of the prophetic sinner and points others by their lives to the God of all mercy.

The mothers and fathers of early Christian asceticism learned to risk everything for the sake of compassion because they had already lost everything in the harsh renunciation demanded by desert life. Their unrelenting theology of the Cross brought them to love by way of death. This, in the end, was the compelling truth they read from the fierce desert landscapes in which they lived.[29]

There is a mercy to be found in the desert that can be found in no other place. Whether it is the desert of the heart or the actual desert that God created to draw these women to himself, it is in the searing heat of fire from the Holy Spirit that conviction and then repentance comes. Repentance, wilderness, longing, desperation, desire, barrenness, boldness, mercy, surrender, exile, intimacy, a prophetic life in the passion of Jesus, and the power of the Holy Spirit are all woven together to form a theology of the desert in which God alone is the focus and the recipient of love. The mercy of God in the lives of these women shows forth the prophetic nature of the wayward heart softened after encountering God's love. The theme of exile and separation continues to cascade down through history.

The fruit of their exile was seen in the intimacy they enjoyed with God. But this intimacy must be shared, because we follow a missionary God. "The disciple is called to follow the Lord not only into the desert and onto the mountain to pray, but also into the valley of tears, where help is needed and onto the cross, where humanity is in agony."[30] This intimacy became contagious and soon others came to drink from their well and to form communities.

The multiplication of communities brought many kinds of women to the desert. Some of them became friaristic in nature and fulfilled their

29. Lane, *Solace of Fierce Landscapes*, 176.
30. McNeill, Morrison, and Nouwen, *Compassion*, 117.

calling from God to go and find those who had not heard of the God who loves, the God who redeems. Ministries unfolded primarily with the poor, the widows, and the orphans. Some returned to the city and others were led back to the desert or villages nearby in order to be of service to others. But even within communities of these women, there was still room for the solitary calling of God.

Even now, in the twenty-first century, there are pockets of the monastic movement found in cloistered form in the tradition of Saint Clare that end the day, praying:

> Mercy, O Lord Mercy! Such mercy as the greatness of our sins and the infiniteness of Your mercy demand. Mercy, O Lord, since mercy is above all your other works. Finally, O Lord, such mercy that we may sincerely repent of all our sins, and that through your mercy they may be blotted out, and we may sing for all eternity the praises of Your tender mercy. Amen![31]

Women who chose to go to the desert in the fourth century chose a life of exile in order to be closer to God. These women who embraced the harshness of living in the desert did so as a response to their sins and a hope of knowing intimacy with God. The lives of the three women who made these choices became filled with prophetic promises for the rest of us who would follow Jesus.

A theology of the desert is seen through repentance, mercy, friendship, and community with others of the same mind as they searched out the ways of God. As communities multiplied and ministries unfolded, those who benefited from a life of exile began to see the fruit of exile. From a women's movement of the desert to the suffrage and women's missionary movement of the nineteenth century we now turn.

Women's Movements: Nineteenth Century

The nineteenth century brought the beginnings of the suffrage movement. Women fought for the right to vote, to preach, and to make their voices heard. As it turned out, Christians were the ones spearheading the movement. The calling was to set women free in all spheres of society, including

---

31. This prayer is often attributed to Saint Francis, but also believed to go back much earlier. I discovered it when I lived in the Monastery of Poor Clares, Santa Barbara, CA, a Franciscan monastery found in many places of the world. No one could remember if they had ever heard it before coming to the monastery.

the church. Much transpired during both the suffrage and the women's missionary movement that would bring gender justice to the forefront.

Suffrage Movement as Springboard

What has become known as an unlikely friendship between Susan B. Anthony and Helen Barrett Montgomery was to have lasting consequences for women throughout history. They worked for the rights of women for many years. Both women lived in Rochester, New York, and came together from a Christian background. They both believed strongly in the cause they were fighting for and led with great vigor as they recruited many women to join them. At one point, Montgomery made it her priority to focus on breaking down the gender barriers within the missionary world. That was her main calling, and so the lives of the two women took different trajectories.

Being outsiders of the male-entrenched system, exile played a large part in both their lives especially in the areas of political clout, power, and the right to choose how to live their lives. They were unwavering in their resolve to break down gender inequity and establish a new way of understanding the rights of women in society. Both Anthony and Montgomery were fighting the injustice against all women. It was a prophetic statement that God was using these two women to sound the alarm for those perpetuating patriarchy, both within and without the church.

The justice frame we talked about earlier is central for understanding the necessity of passionate protest. Lyndi Hewitt and Holly J. McCammon describe three frames (justice, societal reform, and home protection) that they used in the analysis of the suffrage movement: "These frames drew on language from the American Revolution, the Declaration of Independence, and other sources of democratic ideals. In these ways, the justice frame tapped into deeply resonant American values; but in other ways, it represented a radical challenge to prevailing beliefs about the role of women in society. The justice frame held that women should be equal players in politics, with voting rights and thus a formal voice in political affairs."[32]

The justice frame is helpful in seeing why the suffrage movement insisted on equality with men. It is found in the speeches, marches, and civil disobedience of the women. It gave a challenge to women to rise up against the practices of the day and address them systemically. The justice frame calls for radical activity, whereas the other frames only call for reform.

32. Hewitt and McCammon, "Explaining Suffrage Mobilization," 35.

Susan B. Anthony said, "I pray every single second of my life; not on my knees, but with my work. My prayer is to lift woman to equality with man. Work and worship are one with me."[33] Anthony's life was spent working as one of the leaders of the suffrage movement, in hopes of bringing freedom to the women of America. Montgomery chose to spend her life fighting for social reform in order for women to take their rightful place on the mission fields of the world.

It would seem that the suffrage movement at this point in history may have helped to garner support from likeminded women who longed to take the gospel to the ends of the earth. There was a great stirring in the hearts of women not only for the right to vote, but also to preach the good news of salvation. In this way the suffrage movement could be seen as a springboard, a catalyst, or a trigger for Christian women to rise up. Both leaders came from Christian frameworks. Their vision encompassed overlapping spheres of work, activity, and influence. Both movements came from the same source, though the application of God's heart for justice played out in divergent ways.

Women's Missionary Movement

Helen Barrett Montgomery was a great leader in the establishing of a women's missionary movement. The passion that burned within Montgomery is evident in her many books. I have chosen to highlight one of her books that tells the story of the fire in the bellies of women who would not be separated from the needs of desperate women around the world.

In the introduction to her book *Western Women in Eastern Lands*, concerning women's missionary movements in the nineteenth century, Montgomery writes:

> With no militant methods and no thought of increased self-culture and opportunity, hundreds of thousands of women are seeking the uplift of oppressed womanhood and the betterment of social conditions in the most needy places of the world, seeking it in the way and the Spirit of Jesus. Not until all women who love Him and are called by His Name unite in the task can His Kingdom come.[34]

33. Harper, *Life and Work*, 859.
34. Montgomery, *Western Women in Eastern Lands*, xiv.

Montgomery referenced thirteen of the earliest women's mission groups.[35] These were small groups that gathered within their own denomination. Montgomery's part in these groups was as instigator, leader, mentor, and role model. She was also an historian, and as such felt the importance of recording the progress being made in the growth of women's missionary societies. (For a listing of women's missionary societies see appendix B.)

The need for expansive women's missions became obvious. Montgomery documents the words of a young male missionary who had just returned from China due to bad health. She says that his urgent request was revolutionary at the time (1854), when he said, "Men were shut out from ministry by the iron bars of custom that imprisoned women in Zenanas, secluding them from the outside world. The missionary wife at best could only give a fragment of her time and strength to the work; then why not send out women to minister to the uncounted millions of women in non-Christian lands?"[36] The Chinese women wondered why there were no women to come and teach them. Montgomery took up his challenge and sent the word out.

The women came together but were met with opposition from every side. Montgomery likens it to Sanballat and Tobiah coming against Nehemiah as he was trying to build the wall! "The new venture met with scant encouragement. Men and women doubted the practicability and agreed to the impropriety of sending out 'unmarried' females. Many, even of the missionaries were utterly hopeless as to any good being accomplished."[37]

But the women would not be denied and thus the "Society for Promoting Female Education in the East" was formed. Montgomery called it "the oldest of the great missionary boards of women, a society for three-quarters of a century has gone on its ever growing work of blessing. From China to South India, to Ceylon, to North India, to Palestine, to Persia, to South Africa, to Japan, their missionaries have gone; Zenana workers, teachers, physicians, nurses,evangelists, an ever enlarging sisterhood of ministry."[38]

England had responded, but America had not. Montgomery's leadership in women's missions was fraught with opposition. Mission boards so strongly came against a women's missionary movement that after many

35. Ibid., 19.

36. Ibid., 22. A zenana is the part of the house reserved for the women of the household.

37. Ibid., 23.

38. Ibid.

years the movement hit a wall and the endeavor was stalled, but it did not die. Finally, the "Women's Union Missionary Society" was created in 1860. It was the first incorporated women's society and included women from across all denominations. Many women's missionary societies began to grow and flourish throughout both England and America.

At the end of her book, Montgomery sums up the importance of a women's movement in missions. She shares the vision in her interpretation of Ezekiel, as she illustrates the picture of water rising, making the case for two essentials: the words of Christ and the power of Christ being necessary for the mandate of the women's missionary movement to be accomplished. Her summary is a call for priorities and allegiance to be reordered. It is also a challenge to go to the desert in order to bring redemption to those who are lost and oppressed. Montgomery says:

> So many voices are calling us, so many goods demand our allegiance, that we are in danger of forgetting the best. To seek first to bring Christ's Kingdom on the earth, to respond to the need that is sorest, to go out into the desert for that loved and bewildered sheep that the shepherd has missed from the fold, to share all of the privilege with the unprivileged, and happiness with the unhappy, to lay down life if need be, in the way of the Christ, to see the possibility of one redeemed earth, undivided, unvexed, unperplexed, resting in the light of the glorious gospel of the blessed God, this is the mission of the women's missionary movement.[39]

Having given a sketch of the beginnings of the women's missionary movement in the nineteenth century, I found the writings of missiologists Dana Robert and Ruth Tucker most informative. They are perhaps the best at documenting women's church history and Christian movement history. They bring fresh air and life to the topic. Robert says,

> The subordination of women missionaries to male-dominated norms and structures has had important ramifications for mission theory. . . . Put another way, women's mission theory focused either on personal witnessing or on working toward the reign of God. Church planting and the subsequent relationship between church and mission was rarely a part of women's public missiological agenda. Even if women planted mission churches in practice, suitable men took over the pastoral work as soon as possible.[40]

39. Ibid., 278.
40. Robert, *American Women in Mission*, 409–10.

Challenges

What can we learn from both movements? What do the fourth-century desert mothers movement and the nineteenth-century women's missionary movement have in common? Their camaraderie can be seen in the radical nature of their commitment to the cause of Christ. I believe both were inspired by the Holy Spirit and both needed pioneering women to launch out alone, then in small gatherings, then growing into a movement of women desiring to bring change. And both were branded with the exilic nature of the prophetic. For the Desert Mothers it was a change in how the Christians of the day should follow Jesus into the hard places, not only of physical location but also the hardness of their hearts. Never intending to form communities or create a movement, they followed the narrower way to Christ and the rest came later. Additionally, both Susan B. Anthony and Helen Barrett Montgomery had unique roles to play in the nineteenth century. They were both pioneering, fighting for the rights of women to vote, and also fighting to take their rightful place on the mission field.

In one sense, it can be said that both movements energized each other. They gave one another not only the impetus and momentum but instilled in the women bravery and courage in the face of great opposition. Both movements fought for the liberation of women and girls. R. Pierce Beaver made the following statement:

> The Women's Liberation Movement in the United States can in part be traced back to the struggle by church women to participate personally in the overseas mission and to gain an equal place with men in the support and direction of it at the home base. The movement gave women courage to attempt a wide variety of aims and goals within the country and to organize a multitude of societies intended to achieve them. The women's foreign missions movement was thoroughly evangelistic and concerned with saving souls. But its power was generated through dedication to the liberation of women and girls in Oriental and primitive societies. The women were much more adventurous than the men who dominated the general societies and their pioneering forced the denominational boards into policies and programs they might have been very slow to adopt.[41]

Anthony forged a way through a male-dominated society in order to fight for the rights of women to make their voices heard and gain the

41. Beaver, foreword to *Lamps Are For Lighting*, 7.

right to vote. Montgomery labored for women to be a part of gathering the harvest through participation and leadership in the missionary world. She paved the way for women to take their rightful place. But the missions for women were often taken over by men when the way was made smooth. The backlash of the takeover has echoed throughout the missionary world since then. Today, we have the right to vote, but we still have the need for a new women's mission to be forged.

Women of today could take the lessons learned from the struggle for the rights of women and apply them to a fresh expression of women called together for the same purpose. The nineteenth-century women's movements lend instruction, as do the Desert Mothers, who showed it is possible to abide in Jesus with lives of joyful exile that bear uncommon fruit.

Summary

The life lived in exile by the Desert Mothers, after their escape from comfortable Christianity under Constantine's rule, sets a precedent for returning to the authentic ways of the early church. The exilic nature of the formation of monasteries and nunneries shows the need for community in the face of solitary exile. The lessons learned from the rugged ascetic life, tell the stories of women finding redemption in the desert. These women embraced harsh desert living as a response to their commitment to God. Prostitutes of promise were given as examples of signs and wonders for those who would follow in their footsteps. Their choices of emotional, physical, relational, and sometimes spiritual exile became prophetic examples to all who were hungering to know more of God. Mercy was received, community was formed, and ministry was launched as a love offering to God.

The exilic life of the Desert Mothers, as well as the women's missionary movement of the nineteenth century, forged a way for women to choose to take their rightful place in the hard places of the missionary world. This has been a shaping influence for those willing to abandon all for the sake of Christ. Anthony and Montgomery are examples of two women who formed groups of dissent that soon emerged into a movement. Believing that Jesus wants to remake and radicalize today's women in order for many to walk with him in areas of highest risk has been made clear.

Lastly, it is often said that history repeats itself, although nothing in history is an exact replication of things that have happened before. Nevertheless, what was once known as the first women's missionary movement can be used to reflect upon what is necessary today. This indeed sets the historical stage for the next chapter. Exiled women in the early twentieth century tell parts of what they encountered in their walk with God. Their obedience led them to places in the world that were hostile, forsaken, and dangerous.

Six

Historical Pioneer Missionaries

THE LIVES OF A few historical women who made the choice to become missionaries are examined in this chapter. Some of the women are well known (in the missionary community) and others have been lost in archival dust. Their life stories are best told in narrative form in order to introduce the reader to the real story behind the name.

The stories of courage handed down over the years from pioneering missionary women give impetus to the emergence of a women's monastic-missionary/friaristic mission that chooses to live and work in danger zones. My own life has benefited greatly from historical mentoring. The lives of Annie Taylor and Gladys Aylward, as well as Mildred Cable and her comrades Francesca and Evangeline French are proof of the women's audacity and determination to follow after Jesus wherever he leads them.

These particular missionaries were chosen because each faced enormous challenges in their own lives that had to be surmounted. Each one was told she was unqualified in some way. All were told that what they wanted to do was not in the realm of possibility. All three of these women worked in Tibet and so I offer them as examples of pioneering women in the truest sense of the word. What are the issues surrounding the calling of these women? I will paint with broad strokes the stories of their lives in order to show their perseverance to do the will of God no matter what the cost. This is done in narrative form, so that the flavor of their lives hopefully comes through.

Annie Taylor

Of all the pioneering women I have researched, Annie Taylor has made the deepest impression. There is not much known or written about her, but I have been able to rummage through the archives of Overseas Missionary Fellowship and have come up with articles that seem frozen in time. What do we know of Annie Taylor?

She was the first European woman to set foot on Tibetan soil, and to gain entrance into the very heart of Tibet. Annie Royle Taylor was born October 17, 1855, in Cheshire, England. She was frail, unschooled, weakened by heart disease, almost died because of severe bronchitis, and was regarded as a semi-invalid. But she had one thing in her favor, she was stubborn. She came to Christ at the age of thirteen, and this, combined with an old book written about Tibet being a closed country with its strange and mysterious religion, became two of the defining moments in her life.[1] Out of the crucible of suffering God was calling her to the life of a missionary. Motivated by the preaching of John Moffat and challenged to go to the far reaches of the mission field, she was at the same time discouraged to go precisely because she was a woman. Taylor did not listen to the misogyny directed against her call but instead bore through the prejudice.[2]

In 1884, she went to Asia with the China Inland Mission, and after waiting for many years on the India/China border she felt God told her specifically to go quickly into China. From there she and a handful of cohorts waited for the right moment. Again, when the time was right, off they went over the high passes and into Tibet. But she was soon to find out that five people accompanying her were not all friends; one of them turned back, two betrayed her, and another died.

As they crossed over the border, Tibetan robbers attacked Taylor's party and most of their belongings were stolen. She lost all of her extra clothes, her camp supplies, and two horses. Nogby, one of the young men, lost heart as well and turned back to China. Six weeks later, Leucotze died of the cold on a snowy pass. "He was a big, strong-looking man," Taylor said, and continued, "The Master has called to account the strong, and left the weak to go on and claim Tibet in His name."[3]

1. Carey, *Adventures in Tibet*, 146–64.
2. Ibid., 207–13.
3. Ibid., 58.

Betrayed by fellow workers, attacked by bandits, and almost left for dead except for one faithful Tibetan worker, Taylor resolved that nothing would keep her from preaching the gospel in Tibet. On she went, armed with only four books that she kept sewn inside her clothing. The four books were *Daily Light*, the *New Testament and Psalms*, a hymnbook, and a diary in which she kept note of her travels and thoughts as she made her way across the frozen wasteland of Tibet.[4]

At one point in the journey, the little group found themselves among the Goloks, who were then known to be more fierce and warring than the average Tibetan! But as God's providence would have it, the leader of the Goloks at that time was a woman, and she and Taylor got along splendidly. Thus, she was kept safe and protected by the "chieftainess, a woman named Wachu Bumo."[5]

Taylor was arrested on January 3, 1893, just three days short of reaching Lhasa, and was forced to turn back. In seven months of grueling travel she had gone over 1300 miles but the goal of preaching the gospel in Lhasa eluded her. Upon her return to England she said good-bye to the China Inland Mission. She was not easy to get along with and very independent. Maybe because of that or maybe because of God's direct call, Taylor decided to leave the CIM and start her own mission, called the "Tibet Pioneer Mission." However, Hudson Taylor (no relation to Annie) wanted to encourage her and became one of her "referees," what today would be called a board member.[6]

Annie Taylor set up a trader's shop and medical clinic near the Indian border. Taylor and her little band of workers lived in a small town called Yatung, just a few miles inside Tibet in the Chumba Valley. This turned out to be a strategic place to live, as their home was often full of Tibetans, which Taylor welcomed and always told them the story of Jesus dying for them. Along with the Tibetans, she and her coworkers, Bella Ferguson and Mary Foster (two single women who joined the Tibet Pioneer Mission), were able to go in and out of Tibet. When asked about the dangers and rigors of trading in that vast land, she always put her faith in Christ and said that nothing was impossible!

In her small and very rare book *Pioneering in Tibet*, she says, "I went in simple faith, believing that the Lord had called me. I knew that

4. Robson, *Two Lady Missionaries*, 11–112.

5. Lambert, *Missionary Heroes in Asia*, 126.

6. A. Taylor, *Pioneering in Tibet*, 75. For more information on Taylor, see pp. 75–79.

the difficulties were great and that the enemies would be numerous; but I trusted God to take care of me, just as He protected David from the hands of Saul."[7] It was said, "She got not far from Kambajong, a Tibetan fort. Here the natives would ask her frequently what they were to do with her body if she died. She told them she was not going to die just then."[8] However, when they tried to poison her, she did become quite sick, but lived to tell the story.

Bella Ferguson writes one chapter in Taylor's book, "Extracts from Letters" and ends her letter saying,

> And now in my closing letter, I ask you to praise God for thrust-ing me forth as another witness for Jesus into the land so long closed against the Gospel, and for shewing me a little of His work-ing there. Numbers have heard the Gospel for the first time, while quite a few have been healed in the name of Jesus by the laying on of hands in answer to prayer. And I ask you to join dear Miss Taylor and me in definite prayers for the salvation of those who hear, and for me that I may soon be able to speak Tibetan.[9]

Annie Taylor's mission was made up of very strong, individualistic people, and at first fourteen people from England went to join her. I can imagine the excitement, but often they did not get along well and so she urged them to join the CIM instead. Sources say that her little mission be-gan to crumble after about one year.

But Taylor's heart was set on spreading the good news of Jesus in Tibet. Whether she was in China or India, her call to Tibet was strong. In many ways, she was living a life of exile, orchestrated by God. She was waylaid at the Sikkim-Tibet border and became a trader in order to stay among the traveling Tibetans. Taylor's hope of returning to Tibet was quashed be-cause of government regulations and in due time her health went downhill. Sometime after 1907 she returned to England and nothing more is known of her life after Tibet. Nothing has been written concerning the way in which her life ended. Some have said that Taylor was essentially a loner, in-tent on her way, mesmerized by her own vision, and impatient with others. "Looking back on my life," she said, "I see that I have seldom undertaken what everybody else was doing. I have always preferred to strike out a new

---

7. Ibid., 11.

8. Ibid.

9. Ibid., 70.

road and then, when the way was made tolerably smooth, I have left it for others to travel. In this sense, I may consider myself a pioneer."[10]

Taylor wrote an article, "The Degradation of the Women" for *China's Millions*, a magazine published by the China Inland Mission. The date was July 30, 1887, and after describing the conditions of the women around her, she ended the short piece by saying, "The weather here is now very cold, but bright; the climate agrees well with me. I like living alone; God is so near. I feel more and more my nothingness and His omnipotence. God has been blessing me much. He has said, and He will bring it to pass—'I will bless thee, and thou shalt be a blessing.'"[11] This was a life of exile lived to its fullness and she leaves a robust legacy to those with similar callings.

Taylor died alone, with no one knowing where or how or when. Rumors persist, but even the CIM/OMF archives give no clue as to what happened. Nevertheless, she died living her life in obedience to God. It is possible that if she had been part of a friaristic order of likeminded women, she would possibly have been able to do so much more.

An unnamed source in Taylor's book, *Pioneering in Tibet*, said,

> As Livingstone by his great journeys opened the way for the gospel into dark Africa, so our sister expects that God will use her journey to pave the way for missionaries. She believes that the promise stands good: "Every place that the sole of your foot shall tread upon, that have I given unto you"; and in the name of the Lord God she has taken possession of Tibet, fully anticipating that when the right [people] arise to go forward and possess the land the way will be made plain, and the Gospel be published in this hitherto inaccessible region.[12]

This small book written by Annie Taylor is tucked away in the archives of Princeton. In the last few pages she outlines the principles, doctrine, and requirements for any wishing to join the Tibet Pioneer Mission. The requirements for joining the mission were as follows:

> The object of the mission was to evangelize Tibet; the work of the mission would be pioneering, until the objective was reached; the principles of the mission were to be the same as those of the CIM (China Inland Mission); wanted were "true-hearted and humble-minded men and women of God, full of the Holy Spirit and faith,

10. Miller, *Top of the World*, 66.
11. A. Taylor, "Degradation of the Women," 62.
12. A. Taylor, *Pioneering in Tibet*, 18.

experienced in Gospel work"; it was enough for her to trust God alone for her needs and she expected that of others; everything was to be brought before God in prayer, believing that debt was inconsistent with dependence upon God alone; everyone in her mission must have sound, orthodox Christian faith; [they were to] tell of their experiences of being led by the Holy Spirit, as well as the power of prayer.[13]

The challenge Taylor puts forth in these requirements for her mission is the willingness to be exiles, nomads, and pilgrims, refugees of God living out their lives in abandon to the One who sets apart his called ones. The tenor of Taylor's life is layered with exile in her calling to the people of Tibet, the way she went about it, and the people she desired to have with her.

She ends the book by saying, "Brethren and sisters, 'The harvest truly is great, but the labourers are few: pray ye therefore the lord of the harvest, that he would send forth labourers into His harvest,' And continue to pray for Tibet; for God says, 'Ask of Me, and I shall give thee the heathen for thine inheritance, and the uttermost parts of the earth for thy possession.'"[14]

The last page of the book is an "endorsement" by H. Rylands (pastor) and G. H. Rouse D. D., written from Darjeeling, India, in May 1895. They say:

Having seen much of Miss Taylor, and knowing that she has consecrated her life to the evangelization of Tibet, and admiring as we do her faith and zeal, we trust that she will soon secure two or three other devoted women as helpers.

The land for which she pleads must prove one of the most trying fields of Missionary labour; but to those who have the physical and other qualifications for the work, and who are prepared to forget self, and seek only the advancement of the redeemer's Kingdom, there is something specially inspiring in the thought of being pioneers in so hard a field for the sake of Him who left heaven for the cross that He might save us.

They will find that Miss Taylor will not ask them to endure any hardship from which she will herself shrink; and her faith, devotedness, and experience, will be a stimulus to them. But we should especially urge that any who may think of responding to her appeal will carefully COUNT THE COST before-hand, try to put away all romantic ideas of Mission work, and to realize that

13. For Annie Taylor's exact quote see appendix C.
14. A. Taylor, *Pioneering in Tibet*, 78.

work in Tibet means drudgery, privation, frequent disappointment, and patient, persevering toil.[15]

Taylor's life is a great example of courage and perseverance. She would
not quit, in spite of health, harsh conditions, betrayal, loneliness, and falling short of her goal. But she succeeded in following Jesus wherever he led
her. She was determined to reach the Tibetan people with the good news
that would set them free. Her resolve to walk in obedience to the nudges
of the Holy Spirit paved the way for women who had been dissuaded by
others, but knew the unmistakable call of God on their lives.

Annie Taylor leaves us with a high standard. Today, we must ask those
who have a "heart for missions" the same hard questions. Are we convinced
that to follow God's direction is more important than listening to the deter-
rence often coming from those who lack understanding? Are we willing
to embrace the separation that seemed to be her calling? Exile is often the
price to be paid.

Gladys Aylward

Gladys Aylward was a parlor maid from London; a most unlikely prospect
for pioneering missions. Rejected by the China Inland Mission because
she was not "suitable," she knew that God had called her to China and she
would not let go. Trusting God for everything, she bought a one-way ticket
as far as she could go, traveling across Russia in the middle of a war, to meet
up with a woman she had never met, in order to be faithful to the God
whom she loved. She may not have been suitable for the mission societies
of her day, but God wanted her. And she gladly embraced the exile that was
offered to her.[16]

God turned her weakness into strength when he needed someone he
could trust with a hundred Chinese orphans as the Japanese chased them
across high mountain ranges in China. Much has been written about her
and even a movie, *The Inn of the Sixth Happiness*, was made. But not many
know the story of the big impact this small woman had in a large monastery
full of lamas and monks in Tibet.[17]

---

15. Ibid., 79.
16. Thompson, *London Sparrow*, 7–23.
17. Burgess, *Small Woman*.

Once when a few monks were traveling to a small town, the head lama told them to find out where "this God who loved" could possibly live. Many years passed, then one day when they were in the city of Kansu, they asked someone, "Can you tell us where the God who loves lives?"[18] They were pointed to the house of a Chinese evangelist. He gave them the Gospel of Mark, which they took with them and read over and over again. They became fixated on the verse that says to go into all the world and preach the gospel to every creature. And so with great excitement, they waited for the people to come to tell them about Jesus. Finally, after many years the lone monk saw Aylward and her friend, and he was certain that God had sent them!

Aylward was traveling in the Kansu district of far northwestern China, doing survey work, when the Tibetan Buddhist lama came to her. He invited Gladys and her friend to his monastery where they stayed for a number of days. The Tibetan took them to the head lama where they sat for hours, singing the gospel and then teaching. Back and forth, back and forth, this went on for days. But at night, lamas would silently make their way down the halls to their rooms, knock on the doors, and ask them to tell the story of how Jesus had died. This happened night after night; they never tired of hearing about the death of Jesus.

These Tibetan monks wanted to know about the Cross! Not even the signs and wonders, the healings, or the miraculous birth interested them so much as the story of the Cross and the God who laid down his life for them. Aylward and her friend were astonished at the hunger they showed for God. She met with the head lama before they left and he told her the story of how, many years ago, some of the monks were traveling through a small town when they heard a man talking about believing in Jesus, and if they would believe, they would be saved. And not only would they be saved, but it was a free gift! This man gave them a Christian tract, telling of the gospel; the monks took it back to the monastery where they read it over and over again until it fell apart.[19] The lama said that God had sent them to tell of the God who loved. The good news that Aylward brought was the answer to the longing of their hearts.

In the face of ridicule, poverty, war, disdain, and rejection, Aylward knew beyond any doubt that God had called her to China. When the Japanese invaded China, she never wavered. When God led her to climb

18. Tuck, *This is My Story*, 38–39.
19. Ibid., 40–42.

mountains and navigate rivers in order to lead over a hundred children to
safety, she said yes.[20] Many stories of Aylward can be told and need to be
passed on to those who would follow the voice of God to preach the good
news to the lost and those in great need.[21]

Mildred Cable and the French Sisters

Mildred Cable and the French sisters, Evangeline and Francesca, turned
forced exile into a greater understanding of God's way. All three originally
sailed from England in 1928, and chose to give their lives in service to God
in China and beyond. They worked for the China Inland Mission for many
years and spent two decades in Shansi involved in evangelism and education. Just when some said they should retire and take it easy, they made a
momentous decision and determined to go to the least evangelized areas of
China and into greater Tibet.[22]

Many came against them, saying they were middle-aged women,
and what could they possibly do in the back of beyond? "To a good many
people it had seemed not heartrending but just plain foolishness. Why leave
this important and successful school work to go off on some harebrained
scheme of roaming over vast deserts looking for a few isolated tent-dwellers
and remote villages, when there were literally tens of thousands of people
near at hand, all needing to hear the Gospel?"[23]

But against all the concern of others, they headed west and established
a base out of which they worked and traveled. Cable and her two friends
chose this particular town because it was the last place to live inside the
Great Wall; it was also known as the town where all the criminals congre-
gated.[24] They had chosen a life of exile in order to reach those who had not
heard.

From there they proceeded to traverse the Gobi desert and preach
the gospel to all with whom they came in contact. "They uprooted themselves, therefore. They abandoned their homes, their friends; they broke
all the dear familiar fetters which time creates to bind; and, with only such

20. Latham, *Gladys Aylward*, 34–48.

21. Davey, *Never Say Die*, 7–95.

22. Tucker, *Guardians of the Great Commission*, 85–86.

23. Thompson, *Desert Pilgrim*, 11–12.

24. Tucker, *Guardians of the Great Commission*, 85–88.

small personal effects as were strictly necessary, they set out for the Great Northwest—Kansu."[25]

Because of their obedience, these wandering pioneer women led by the Holy Spirit in the hinterlands of Tibet were able to bring Jesus to a lost and demonized lama of the Red Hat Sect. From that time forward, "In the folds of his red shawl he now always carried a copy of the New Testament, the Book of Emancipation, the Word which proclaimed his redemption from the service of Satan and his release from the remorseless revolutions of the Wheel of Reincarnation."[26]

In the closing pages of this small book, *The Red Lama,* these tough and persistent missionaries document the state and the statistics of Tibet at that time in 1932. (Today, it is not much different; less than one percent are Christian.) At the close of their book, Cable and Francesca French exhort all who will listen, "Volunteers who are afraid to expose themselves to hardship and even danger need not apply for Tibet."[27]

These three women leave a legacy to women of any age that where God calls, nothing said by men can hold them back. The only hindrance would be of their own making and that would be their refusal to walk in obedience to God.

Susie Rijnhart, MD

Lastly, one of the women who sacrificed much in her missionary work in Tibet was Susie Carson Rijnhart. Born in 1868, in Chatham, Ontario, she graduated at the top of her class in medical school. Not long after, she met and married Petrus Rijnhart after hearing him speak on the great evangelistic need in Tibet. She was a Canadian physician, and as there was great need for medical help overseas, they soon hit the high road from North America to the wastelands of Tibet. They set up a small clinic and began to live out the gospel as well as preach the good news to the Tibetans and Chinese.[28]

They determined to go further into the deep interior of Tibet. During this initial venture to the high places, Rijnhart lost her husband and child in the rugged Himalayas, yet remained determined to bring Christ to the lost

25. Tiltman, *God's Adventurers*, 32–33.

26. Cable and F. French, *Red Lama*, 32.

27. Ibid., 44.

28. Robson, *Two Lady Missionaries*.

ones of Tibet. In her book *With the Tibetans in Tent and Temple*, written in 1902, Rijnhart says,

> Kind Christian friends have questioned our wisdom in entering Tibet. Why not have waited, they ask, until Tibet was opened by "the powers" so that missionaries could go in under government protection? There is much heart in that question, but little logic. Christ does not tell his disciples to wait but to go.

> We are not to choose conditions, we are to meet them. The early apostles did not wait until the Roman Empire was "opened" before they kindled the fire that "burned to the water's edge all around the Mediterranean," but carrying their lives in their hands they traveled through the cities of Asia Minor, Greece and finally to Rome, delivering their message in the very centers of paganism. Persecutions came upon them from every side, but nothing but death could hinder their progress or silence their message. They went to glorious martyrdom and being dead they have never ceased to speak.[29]

Rijnhart returned to the West and spent four years at home in Canada, attempting to heal from all the agony, pain, and broken health she had experienced in Tibet. She began to build a new life at home, but then looked toward the East one more time. She was determined to go back to Tibet, to fulfill the calling on her life, and she did. After arriving back in China Rijnhart soon married again, to Carson Moyes, a missionary with the China Inland Mission. They were determined to remain in the country but Rijnhart's health had so deteriorated they made the decision to return to Canada. Three weeks after she gave birth to her new baby boy, she went to be with the Lord. She died for Tibet by giving her life in exile for the people she loved.[30]

And There Were Others

And there were others whose names were not written down in the historical records for all to see. They will not be mentioned here. Some of them chose a life of exile in order to spend their lives in remote regions, in far-away lands, hidden in that place of the Spirit, where only God knows their

---

29. Rijnhart, *With the Tibetans*, 395.
30. Robson, *Two Lady Missionaries*, 153–60.

personal exploits and adventures. The author of Hebrews mentions the fact of their suffering as they followed after the Lamb:

> . . . and others experienced mockings and scourgings, yes, also, chains and imprisonments. They were stoned, they were sawn in two, they were tempted, they were put to death with the sword; they went about in sheepskins, being destitute, afflicted, ill-treated (people of whom the world was not worthy), wandering in deserts and mountains and caves and holes in the ground. . . (Heb 12:36–38)

Indeed, there are a few right now who have made choices to live in relative obscurity and be known only by the One who has sent them. It is enough that God alone knows and that he is the One who has given them power not only to heal the sick, cleanse the lepers, and to bring the word of redeeming love to those in the unreached nomad tents of faraway Tibet, but also to lay down their lives for the sake of his name.

Findings

All of the women were born in the late nineteenth century and all were British, except for one Canadian. All had some connection with the China Inland Mission, although it was not always positive. Except for Susie Rijnhart, who was a medical doctor from Canada, education was varied. Gladys Aylward was a parlor maid and had no formal education. Annie Taylor remained unschooled until she was a teenager because of poor health. Mildred Cable did have advanced education and initially went to China with an established mission.

Concerning awareness of social justice issues, most of the social responsiveness of these historical women occurred in the midst of evangelization. They would not have used the phrase "social justice issues," but they most certainly were moving in the name of Jesus to relieve pain and suffering and injustice among those in their midst. Earthquakes in Tibet kept them involved in ways they would never have imagined before they left England or Canada. Tending to the wounded was so often the way to be the hands and feet of Jesus. Caring for the sick and desperate people they met along the side of the road would today be called a type of justice response to great needs, with a scriptural example being the story of the Good Samaritan (Luke 10:25–37).

The main motivating force in each woman's life was a passion to take the gospel message to the lost; Jesus was their all-consuming desire. Much of the resistance came from those inside the camp (the missionary community and/or church) rather than outside. Each one believed that friendship with God was not only possible but was essential if they were to finish the work he had called them to do.

Taylor and Aylward both worked primarily alone, although they attempted to form teams and carry the liberating word of Christ together with others of like mind. But it seems that God had other plans. Mildred Cable and the French Sisters, commonly called "the Trio," were grateful to have each other as friends and comrades. Rijnhart first went to Tibet with her husband, who was killed, but then returned to carry out the work God assigned to her.

Cable and the French sisters had worked with the China Inland Mission for years before they sensed God calling them to evangelize the far frontier of the Gobi desert. Originally they felt welcomed and a part of the CIM family, but when they decided to strike out on their own, they were met with mocking, discouragement, and ultimately, rejection on the part of many. This was a crucible event in their lives. On one hand they chose their geographical exile, but the emotional exile was thrust upon them.[31]

Taylor was also accepted into the CIM early on, but it became clear that her pioneering heart was meant to travel into Tibet. Her writings give evidence that she experienced exile on many levels—emotional, mental, spiritual, and geographical—and that she had experienced one crucible event after another, spanning much of her life.

Aylward was rejected by the CIM and made her own way to China through Russia during wartime in order to work with a woman whom she did not know and did not want her—all for the love of China that God had put in her heart.[32] She experienced deep rejection as well as exile at every stage of her journey. As each event could be described as a crucible, she chose the high road and embraced the hard choices she must make. But it made her into the woman God called her to be.

Rijnhart knew exile on at least two levels: (1) being called to Tibet (geographic); (2) the death of her husband and baby (emotional and probably spiritual); and then returning to Tibet. The death of her husband and child was obviously a crucible time in Rijnhart's life, but she determined to

31. See Cable, E. French, and F. French, *Desert Journal*.
32. Thompson, *London Sparrow*, 7–23.

forge ahead with her ministry work in Tibet. She chose to lay down her life for the gospel in many ways.

Exile brought each one of these women closer to Jesus in ways they could never have thought possible if they had stayed in the comfort of their known surroundings and familiar relationships. Their hunger for intimacy with God and his purposes led them into places that few others would go. Having said that, my contention is that forming an intentional community of likeminded women called to not only intimacy with God but also to preaching the gospel is an important consideration for today.

Summary

The lives of Annie Taylor, Gladys Aylward, Mildred Cable, Evangeline French, Francesca French, and Susie Rijnhart reveal their depth of resilience and resolve when faced with adversity. Each woman knew exile in some form and each woman was forged in the fires of crucible events.

Taylor met with rejection, but was determined to reach Lhasa when everyone ultimately had failed her. Aylward was tenacious in her calling to China, as she met with much disappointment and intense rejection from many sources. She made the decision to follow hard after God in the midst of war, relationship angst, and ill health. Mildred Cable and her friends the French sisters embraced a life lived out in exile when they left familiar surroundings for a new adventure with God in remote and unreached areas of China. They received no emotional support and were indeed scorned for their decision to choose the unknown as they were growing older. Susie Rijnhart was deeply misunderstood as she turned once again to face the brutal land of Tibet after losing both her husband and child. Her unrelenting faith gave her authority to speak with a prophetic voice to the church, to those Christians who did not act on their beliefs, but continued to wait. She admonished the church to rise up and go because time was rushing past them. Not waiting for comrades to join her, she carried on with the mission that God asked of her.

The legacies left by these women serve as a model of inner resolve and deep faith for today. Rather than waiting endlessly, they made the decision to move in rhythm with the Holy Spirit's prodding. These women paid the price of exile, and each made the decision to take up the individual cross especially designed for her as she followed hard after God. Their stories beckon us to look back at how some of our foremothers responded to the nudge of God and how this could be applied in a community setting today. Their tenacity and grit in the face of exile is a gift to those women waiting for the exact "call of God."

The stories of our missionary foremothers lead us to the next chapter, which looks at the lives of contemporary women pioneers and what they have to say. Although history has moved on, the principles and guidance of scripture remain the same.

SEVEN
_____

Contemporary Pioneer Missionaries

THIS CHAPTER EXAMINES THE research data obtained from twenty-two contemporary women missionaries interviewed using an open-ended set of interview questions. (For an overview see appendix A.) The stories of three remarkable women are recounted as illustrative of individuals whose present-day lives on the mission field bring a fresh understanding of the meaning of exile.

Research

Pioneering women are pursuing much of the work in closed or hard-to-access countries. Of the twenty-two women participating in the interviews, P#1–22, all were living in high-risk areas in Asia or Africa.[1] The scope of the interview questions was designed to give as thorough an understanding of each woman as possible. Four sets of introductory questions provided information concerning age, geographical areas of work, types of mission work, and access to countries. The key themes of crucible, justice, exile, and gender discrimination—components often found in the radicalization process—are discussed.

The age range of the interviewees spanned fifty-four years with the oldest woman born in 1925 and the youngest in 1979. There were seven

1. The numbering system for identifying the participants in this study was simple. I alphabetized the names of the participants and then gave each a number (e.g., P#1, P#2, etc.) Because of the nature and place of their work and ministry, the women asked for and were promised anonymity. Any personal communication via email or otherwise is noted.

Americans, four Australians, four British, one Canadian, two Dutch, two New Zealanders, one Swazi, and one Swiss and all were involved in cross-cultural ministry of some kind.

Twelve of the women interviewed were single and ten were married. My original intent was to interview only single women but I readjusted my strategy when I realized that many of the married missionary women who live in high-risk areas also had much to contribute regarding the issues of exile and justice.

All those interviewed are missionaries in no-access countries, limited-access countries, or dangerous areas. These women are either working with the poor, engaged in child soldier rescue, offering education and disciple-ship, helping Internally Displaced Persons (IDPs) in war zones, rescuing orphans, or doing advocacy work on behalf of the oppressed. In areas where people have no access to the Bible, there are also many missionaries who are translating scripture into mother-tongue languages. All areas of ministry have a measure of exile that embeds itself into a person's life.

A majority of the women interviewed (twelve of twenty-two) were working in diverse parts of Asia. There are many limited-access countries, as well as war zones within these various countries. Everyone interviewed was doing the work of an evangelist, but in different capacities. Most believe that evangelism and social justice issues must go hand in hand and some of the women expressed this through medical work, relief action, or education. Many of the categories overlapped. One pattern showed itself clearly in that most of the women were called to high-risk areas. Although there were three women who worked in complete-access countries, they were nevertheless involved in activity where risk was involved, such as anti-trafficking and the education of orphans.

Out of twenty-two women, nineteen had chosen to work in limited-access areas where there was definite risk; five were working in war zones where there is obvious danger. The question most often asked is, "Why?" For most women, deep conversion often led to a longing to walk closely in the way of life that Jesus exemplified. Danger in areas where unknown people wait for rescue both physically and spiritually was seen as a natural response. The decision was made out of gratitude for God's mercy.

The Sacred Place of Exile

Crucible Experience

The women had experienced types of crucible events that were often life-changing happenings that required that hard choices be made. Of the twenty-two women interviewed, nineteen said that one of the main crucibles in their life was their conversion to Christ. For them, friends, allegiances, and choices about how they spent their time changed dramatically. Without exception, each woman interviewed said that it was either becoming a Christian or experiencing the baptism of the Holy Spirit that was the defining moment in her life.

Crucible events often occurred after coming to Christ and persecution from family members or friends was common. The women experienced rejection as profound lifestyle changes took place. Allegiances took a different form and friends often changed. Whatever the intense crucible life-changing time (or times) that took place, each event drove the woman to seek God on deeper levels. Frequently, they made choices to become more deeply involved in missionary work.

Eight participants said that experiencing the Holy Spirit was also a life-defining event. Many of the women came from broken, dysfunctional backgrounds and most had experienced some type of emotional or physical trauma in their lives. Still others had known suffering in a number of other areas, including, rejection, abandonment, and abuse. But after encountering the power of the Holy Spirit, their lives took a dramatic turn and the result was confidence, gratitude, and joy.

One woman, P#7, had been held captive and brutally raped by guerilla soldiers during the Congo rebellion in 1964–1965. She is an amazing woman and I was privileged to be able to interview her. Asked if her lifestyle choices changed after that crucible event, she responded,

> God challenged me: "Can you thank Me for trusting you with this experience even if I never tell you why?" My love for Him became more utterly unquestioning—I just knew He was in charge, and I could trust Him no matter what. I have ceased to ask "Why?"

Her decision to continue trusting God with all of her life, no matter the consequence, was certain.

Another woman, P#4, described her first crucible event when her own mother threw her out of her home and onto the streets of her town when she was only a child. She gained wisdom as she had to figure out how to live after the rejection and abandonment. She came to Christ and the church became her home in many ways. Much later, she experienced "massive spiritual abuse in [her] church back home." Even now, as a missionary, she says, "nothing much draws me to church anymore." But she works with para-church organizations on occasion and is committed to fighting for displaced people and against poverty. Crucible events have the potential to be the catalytic experience that ignites change.

Social Justice Awareness

Six categories of social justice issues were examined, including class, race, gender, poverty, people with AIDS, and refugee/IDPs. The women were asked when they first remembered being aware of injustice and what kind of bias, inequality, or prejudice they perceived.

The patterns show that most of the women became aware of justice issues in their youth and in their twenties. Participant #2 remarked, "I have seen discrimination during all of my years at school and in work environments." According to the women, personal experiences and/or watching others being marginalized brought about this new consciousness.

Viewing life from a personal perspective and therefore answering questions from that viewpoint is a natural human response. However, it is interesting to note that women who work in particularly high-risk areas looked at the questions from the perspective of oppressed peoples such as the Karen people of Burma, who are running through the jungle trying to escape from the Burma army. Participant #2 said the following:

> I admire the women of Burma who were born in an area of intense and high-risk activity and chose to stay or go back into those areas despite the dangers. I think they have a great strength and many have a dependence on God that brings courage into these difficult situations. I think that anyone, woman or man, can go into areas like that if they don't let fear stop them from doing what they are called to do, or what they believe is just and right.

Participant #22 is a nurse working in the jungles of Burma. She has been there for a few years now, but had quite a hard time in the beginning. She related to me how she felt about suffering.

> I had a hard time a few years ago. I was very angry at God on behalf of the suffering, violence and injustice in Burma. I have always known God to be good, seeing His grace in my life. But I couldn't see his goodness in Burma. One week, He introduced me

to three people who had suffered horribly fleeing from the Burma army, lost a leg from a landmine and lost a home to the Burma army burning it down. They ALL said that God was good—even though terrible things had happened to them. God had the people of Burma defend his goodness to me. I believe that God is good with all my heart—even though there is suffering. I also believe that anytime someone is afflicted with pain and suffering, it is the same as afflicting that pain on our Lord and Savior. (When you do it to the least of these, you do it to Me.)

Results of the refugee/IDP category of the interview showed that many of the women who are involved in this type of work did not have an awareness of the issue early on. There were only eleven women doing this type of work and all learned about the ravages of war and poverty through awareness once they arrived in the surrounding area or country.

In the midst of danger and suffering, issues of race, class, and gender continued to play a dominant role in how these women responded to situations, not only from their own experience but also by the women they live among. When discussing frames and lenses in an earlier chapter, I demonstrated that it is through gender that reality is viewed. The foundational lens is gender, with the other two being class and race. But gender bias was overwhelmingly the main justice issue that needed to be addressed.

Gender Discrimination

As stated above, the issue of gender discrimination cuts a broad swath through both race and class. The participants in the interview made that clear. Participant #9 brought up the part her family played in her first experience of gender discrimination: "I've never felt so consistently undermined as I have with my own father." This was also true of others.

Sexism was not only acknowledged but encountered by almost everyone. Each woman gave examples of sexist behavior/gender discrimination in various areas of their lives. The fact that many had had their first experience of gender discrimination in the church grabbed my attention from the beginning. For example, when asked when she first became aware of gender discrimination, P#4 said, "In the church!!! Since I started to go there in my teens and my awareness [experience] of it grew substantiality the more I developed into the woman I am today." Participant #3 also commented,

"I became angry at the way women are discriminated against, especially having experienced it myself first hand from the church."

A missionary who works primarily in Africa, P#15, indicated that she became aware of gender discrimination, "When I became a Christian, it was male-oriented leadership and control. I was a thorn in their [church] flesh, as I went to the men-only Bible school and planted churches. Since then, they have made changes to their theology and thankfully changes for the better for women that come after me." This is an example of one woman who served as a pioneer in her situation and leads the way for others to have less resistance.

During the interview process these women quickly made it apparent that along with a strong call from God to go to the mission field, there was also the hope that their giftings would be put to better use outside of their home/church environment. Sadly, this was rarely the case. One of the women I interviewed, P#18, works in a high-risk area and had much to say regarding the lack of gender justice on the present-day mission field. She made the following comments:

> These gender attitudes hinder both married and single women. The whole of the missionary body is hurting and weak because of this issue. These issues of gender coupled with the issues of authority, power and control make addressing this issue even more difficult. Then add to this the prevailing attitude that the man is the autocratic king of his house and marriage and we have an even more toxic combination. Finally, put such a man in authority or a leadership "position" in a mission organization and you have an entrenched mentality that is nearly impossible to dislodge. Most mission organizations are unwilling to address this issue because they are theologically bent on gender issues.

Several women gave examples of gender injustice that are being perpetrated on the women in the mission field right now (P#2, 4, 10, 13, and 20). One woman believes there needs to be another reformation within the church, so that when women are sent out as missionaries they are sent in the fullness of their calling. When talking about leadership on the field, P#18 said, "There is an overemphasis of finding influential men in the culture and then trying to evangelize them to the exclusion of women. This is because of a prevailing attitude that we mainly want to evangelize potential leaders, and women can't be leaders."

Her statement is as strong as it is clear: "Chauvinistic mission boards will bear fruit in kind: chauvinistic church plants." She makes the strong point, "Unless some of these gifted and 'qualified' women are willing to fight the battle, they will not be able to contribute to a change in the presently gender biased organizations, and may never see all their sisters empowered to be and do all that the Father intended for them on the mission field." She ends the communication with me by saying, "At some point there needs to be a movement in missions." She brought up the need for reformation in the church and therefore deep change within the missionary community.

Whether they realized it or not, all of the women were involved in some kind of social justice work or ministry. All of them believe that justice is a part of evangelism; one without the other does not make for a holistic gospel.

Exile

The types of exile the interviewees experienced and whether the exile was perceived, forced, or chosen are important. Five different kinds of exile were discovered in the interviews— geographical, physical, political, emotional, and spiritual—and the fruit of exile became apparent as the participants chose either to retreat when exiled, to resist exile, or to be radicalized by exile.

Most of the women knew when they were experiencing exile, but others only realized it in hindsight. Participant #1 said that she had to go back and forth between her home country and Hong Kong for many years. And after finally returning to live in Hong Kong, she said it was "a phenomenal experience of unknowing exile in retrospect." She now had the words to explain the dynamic of feeling separated.

Participant #14 told me that her exile had been forced at times and chosen at others. She said that "exile in the church was a surprise" and that it was the most painful. She went on to say in later discussion that "exile is what happens for everyone who is on mission with God."

One of the ways that P#13 experienced exile was "after falling in love with a woman and leaving my husband due to shame and guilt. The church I had been attending totally abandoned me, 'handed me over to the devil.' I experienced condemnation and gossip to a terrible extent. Exiled from church . . . "

Another woman, P#3, said she had most definitely experienced exile. "When I was not walking with the Lord, it was me trying to escape the exile." She went on to say, "For me these exile times are constant in my life and are part of my walk, and all my decisions have come from this place. It is in this sacred place, where we are radicalized by God's love—it moves us to action." Participant #9 said, "We are an exile people!" She seemed surprised that I should even think exile is an issue up for discussion. Others expressed the same viewpoint.

Radical Understanding

Because crucible events and exile experience often pointed to a radicalization process that was significant, the following questions were asked:

1. Do you believe that exile played a part in your radicalization process?
2. How would you define radical?
3. Would you consider yourself radical?
4. What kind of woman do you think is drawn to work in selected areas of high risk?

Many of the women in this study that are considered radical in their choices and lifestyles would not necessarily define themselves as radical. Mostly they believe that it is a natural response to the relationship that came out of initial and subsequent encounters with God. For them it does not seem odd or strange but is a love response to the redeeming power of God. Those women who found Christ in the midst of an intense crucible experience were more likely to embrace social justice issues than others. The extension of their conversion showed itself through working among the poor, liberating child soldiers, and then educating and discipling these young victims of conflict. Others are helping Internally Displaced Persons (IDPs) in war zones, rescuing orphans, doing advocacy work on behalf of those suffering from various types of oppression, or translating the Bible into mother-tongue languages.

Those who had experienced marginalization, suffering, or abuse in their lives prior to encountering Christ tended to see Jesus as liberator, feminist, and friend. There was a level of compassion brought to the ministry that was not necessarily present with those who had not known much suffering in their lives.

Participants were asked to give their definitions for the word "radical" or "radicalized woman." After doing so, some women commented that they were more discreetly radical. Participant #11 said, "I am more quietly radical and no longer expect that I will have fellow travelers on the way. It's often a pretty lonely journey. So, in a way, exile has now become a way of life in order to continue to be radical."

Participant #4 defined radical as, "A woman who gives herself single-handedly to a specific cause no matter what the cost and no matter if she fits into the system/norms or not, courage to go against the tide." Another woman, P#20, said that a radical was, "A woman who chooses to act in such a way that well-entrenched systems are required to change."

Two of the women talked about themselves as being radical. Participant #21 said, "I am pretty radical, at least in the eyes of people back in the US. Even colleagues in Africa told me there was no way I could live at a cattle-post for a month—let alone three years. Government workers in [the country] where I worked always thought I was radical. People within my organization think I am pretty radical." Participant #22 offered her thoughts: "Some people may consider me a radical woman. I did leave my nursing job to move to SE Asia with my thirteen-year-old daughter as a single mom to help people in war-torn Burma. I now spend much of my time sleeping on a wood floor, under a mosquito net, eating rice three times a day, so I can do healthcare training for people who will take hope and health to their people in Burma. For me, I feel normal. This is my niche. This is what God created me for. So, I don't feel radical. I feel alive, and I feel like I'm doing what God made me for."

The radicalization process these women experienced gave the following results: (1) some were more quiet in their radicalism than others; (2) some were not willing to call themselves radical, although friends and colleagues often did; and (3) those who did consider themselves radical were working in danger zones. The general consensus on what makes up a radicalized woman is one who is totally sold out, who gives everything she has to follow Christ, no matter what the cost. As these ideas ran through many of the interviews, three women's lives stood out and became prominent, so their stories are told here.

Three Women

Three stories of remarkable women who live in high-risk areas or war zones in Asia are highlighted. The reason for choosing these women is that they represent three different types of exile, whereas the other women interviewed fall into one or more of these definitions of exile. The three women live in China, Burma, and Tibet. For their safety I refer to them using first name pseudonyms: Lydia, Miriam, and Naomi.

Lydia

Lydia felt very independent even at the age of four, and said she has always been aware of the presence of God. Growing up in a Christian household, her parents were missionaries and her grandparents known for their leadership in the body of Christ. But her life was not without trauma in her early years. There were crucible moments and times of feeling abandonment and rejection.

Lydia's home was a country in the Commonwealth until she made the decision to move with her parents to another country, as she felt that was what God was asking her to do. She began to have "excruciating mental distress" and was later shown that it was culture shock. She said, "That bout with culture shock was so bad that nothing in any country or any culture has ever rivaled it since!" This was a crucible moment in her life.

Later, while living in an Asian country, about to embark with a team of colleagues to work in China, one by one the team fell apart, leaving Lydia alone to travel into the interior of China on her own. This proved to be a defining moment in her life as she began to trust God in deeper ways as her provider. Another crucible was formed when she was falsely accused of an inappropriate relationship and was forced to leave the country. She was later vindicated as the Lord fought for justice on her behalf. She returned to China with greater resolve and intimacy with the Lord.

When asked if these crucible times caused changes in her lifestyle choices, Lydia answered, "No, but they have certainly taken me deeper in my relationship with the Lord and increased my level of thanksgiving for all his mercies!"

Concerning justice issues, Lydia has never considered herself a feminist, but in many ways her life speaks differently. Lydia is passionate about "the right for women to have equal educational opportunities as men" and secondly, about "the right for all children to have the opportunity to attend school" in China. Her life as a woman is one that speaks of forging ahead in the face of much conflict.

Lydia believes that getting to the root of something is what it means to be a disciple of Jesus. She believes "a radical is someone who lives one hundred percent to please the Lord Jesus Christ and not for the approval of others. I aspire to this description, but still have a long way to go, as my obedience to Christ is still somewhat tempered by what others might think of me."

When discussing exile, at first Lydia said she didn't think she had ever experienced exile in any extreme. But as she continued on, she related stories of being misunderstood, separated, left alone or by herself in a number of situations, and feeling the rejection as fierce. On one occasion when being totally misunderstood, she felt forced to leave China and experienced intense rejection; she said it was God, through circumstances, who led her into exile. Walking out a life of exile became accepted as part of her commitment to follow Jesus.

Being called names like "lone ranger" and the lack of inclusion within a missionary community are ways an independent missionary can feel misunderstood and rejected. Lydia has had to embrace a lonely exile because of accepting God's call on her life, but said she would never change a thing because it brought her closer to God.

The exile Lydia experienced was partly geographical, emotional, and spiritual. In the face of pain and separation, she chose not to resist or run. Instead she responded by embracing the different forms of exile in order to be radicalized by God. She remains thankful to God for all that happened, as intimacy developed and she grew in her relationship with God, specifically because of the exile.

Miriam

Miriam's life in Burma consists of spending most of her time in the jungle doing work among people who are on the run from the Burma army. Her life is one of being constantly in danger, but knowing that her life is in God's hands. Her determination to know God is what takes her into war zones. She is "uniquely involved with fighting racial discrimination and the unfair treatment of IDPs in Burma." She explained, "There are many examples in the Bible where God is angered by injustice . . . people choosing not to 'do good to the poor, the widow, the orphan and the foreigner.'"

When asked if there was a cause she is passionate about, Miriam said, "I am passionately against the oppression of IDPs by the Burma army, and also the harsh treatment of refugees. These people work very hard to try to earn a living and are chased out of their homes and land. The unfairness and the cruelty of it spurs me into action."

Defining the word "radical" was not at all hard for Miriam:

> Being a radical is to leave the status quo and challenge the way the majority thinks or acts. I do see myself as radical because I've left the American lifestyle of trying to make money and have status. Instead, I am willing to live humbly in order to do the work I do and try to help others. As a woman, often times people think I am crazy to make myself vulnerable like this. Many friends and family don't quite understand this, but I am determined to keep on. I had a few good professors who modeled for me how to be a strong woman and to go forward in my calling without being distracted or dissuaded by others.

When comparing female and male leaders, she had this to say: "Radicalized women have made huge impacts on my life and my view of my abilities. Women tend to have a nurturing ability that encourages her followers and makes more strong radicals. The tendency of a radical male leader is to attract followers, but when the radical male leader is captured; his followers may falter because they were counting on his strength."

I asked her, if she could be any woman in history, who it would be. Miriam replied, "I can't think of anyone in particular. I'd like to be someone who was an ordinary woman good at inspiring others, who wasn't afraid to stand up to injustice and who left the world a better place than she found it."

Concerning exile, Miriam told of how she came to Southeast Asia with a certain mission organization and, after a while, much misunderstanding and conflict ensued. Deciding to leave a particular group of people was part of the exile she experienced and she said it was both forced and chosen. "That period of exile led me to seek my worth in God instead of in the praise of other people. I learned that God is faithful. In the end, by leaving that one community into another, God provided people for my life that were such a blessing and like family. I knew I was exactly where he wanted me to be." She went on to say, "Being exiled helped me take that one last step to lean entirely on God and be less influenced by what my community thinks of me."

Miriam's life lived in the midst of horrific oppression against the ethnic hill-tribe people of Burma is an example of what can be done by one person who takes the word of God seriously. Her exile spreads across geographical, emotional, and physical boundaries. Miriam made hard choices to embrace all that came her way and in the process a deeper faith in God's provision has grown.

Naomi

Naomi is spending her life among Tibetan nomads, bringing the incarnational Christ to those who have never heard. She belongs to a mission organization and is also married. (She and her husband are of the same mind regarding the issues that I write about in her story.) She comes from a British background, basically felt nurtured growing up in a Christian home, and is focused on bringing the unreached to Christ.

An activist not just at heart but in exploits as well, Naomi became aware of gender discrimination at a young age.

> I would hear things like, "girls aren't allowed to do that, girls can't do such and such, soccer teams are only for boys, girls don't become paramedics, girls have to behave a certain way, but boys don't, and so on." Ever since, I have championed the cause of women, any opportunity I had, and tried to help individual women God has put in my life, to rise above their circumstances, particularly if they were oppressed or discounted.

When asked to describe a radical woman, Naomi replied,

> I believe that a truly radical woman is one who follows Jesus with her whole heart and being, and who will embrace His full calling on her life, regardless of the expectations of others and regardless of the risk, trusting that she can do all things through Jesus who strengthens her, and who is not limited by her gender! This is a woman who is not afraid to develop and use her spiritual gifts and her talents and intelligence, even if others don't think it is her prerogative. I have fought with every ounce of my being for the rights of women I have known personally, who were in jeopardy of losing their futures, by virtue of the fact that they are women, living in a sexist environment.

A few of the people who have inspired Naomi include Martin Luther King Jr. in the fight for civil rights, Mary Slessor in Africa, Amy Carmichael in India, and women of the suffrage movement in the nineteenth century. Naomi gains motivation and encouragement from many missionaries who have fought for justice in the lands where they were called. She was mentored by many who serve as examples of those who had known exile of one type or another. Out of their exile she chose to dwell among Tibetan nomads who live in an extreme form of exile.

On the topic of radicalized women, Naomi had this to say:

> The woman who is "radicalized" by Christ, who is truly free in Christ, could potentially have a very unique and very important part to play, if she is willing to be sold out to Christ and to serving others and to standing up for truth and justice, even if it poses a risk to herself. This unique role, however, may not be political or start a powerful movement. It all depends on the sphere of influence that God puts her in, and the task He gives her to do. I think there is many an unsung heroine who is serving the Lord with courage, and touching lives for eternity, by bringing freedom, healing and truth, in her own small corner of the world. The "world" may never know what she's done, but her works and the fruit of her works will live on for eternity, when many another's work will be burned up like so much chaff.

One of the crucible moments in Naomi's life was watching a missionary presentation at her church. "We saw slides of starving people in some third world country. I was particularly touched by the plight of the children. I cried out in my heart, 'God, why doesn't somebody do something?' Immediately he spoke to me, an audible voice in my head, 'Why don't you do something?' I knew from that moment on that I was called to give my life to overseas service, in his name."

Naomi is passionate about women's issues and also about the rights and needs of children. "I hope I will take every opportunity God personally gives me, for being an advocate and a helper in these situations. I would rather take action when I can, than just sit around and talk about it. However, I believe that I have a higher call even than this, on my life, and that is to share the good news of Christ to a lost and dying world." More of her thoughts and observations are highlighted later.

Naomi has known exile geographically and emotionally. As a woman who sees the oppression of women in many spheres, she could be called an outsider in that she aligns herself with outsiders. The choices made in the face of preferential treatment toward men in her particular mission organization have been hard fought. Her choice not to remain silent has made her a role model for women who refuse to give up.

Throughout the gathering of information it became clear that struggle with existing missionary organizations or missionary colleagues often resulted in exile. Often crucibles were formed in the midst of the conflict, and radicalization took on a new dimension as resolve was deepened.

Another missionary woman uses the life of lament to describe the face of exile. Her story is one of deep exile and one that is worthy of telling. It introduces the topics of godly leverage and the prophetic role of missiology. Her story can be found in appendix F.

Summary

Most of the women interviewed grew up in different cultures, but their responses were similar. For many of these women there was a definite paradigm shift in the midst of their own personal crucible(s). Their relationship with God was deepened as the change in their thinking was replaced with a reference point other than themselves. As the shift happened, they began to see with new vision what God had planned for them.

Each woman defines "radical" in a different way, as some of them only see the word or concept in a negative, media-driven, or dictionary-defined way. But a few of the women regard radical as going to the root of something, getting underneath and finding the core truth. A radical is one who goes against the grain for a cause greater than herself. She pursues what others think is impossible and embraces exile as a way of life. She is a woman who chooses to get to the root of a problem or situation in order to change situations or systems. This was true of most, but especially true of those who worked in dangerous areas.

The women who were involved in war zones and/or high-risk regions all aligned themselves with the people they were helping. There was a marked difference in how they perceived their relationship with God and others. For example, they tended to answer the questions in solidarity with the people in the limited-access country or the war zone where they worked. They were not focused on themselves. Often, the crucible experiences of those in need became their own crucible. They chose to experience the pain of others as if it was their own. These women who worked overseas were other-centered and could understand the exile of those in war ravaged countries, because of their own separation and exile.

As the women poured out their answers to my questions, it became evident that in order for pioneering work to take place, each woman had to experience some type of exile in her life. This was often for an extended period of time ranging from a year to a lifetime. The more rugged the environment of ministry, the more intense the quality of exile experienced. No one experiencing the tougher rigors of exile would have it any other way, because not only of what was accomplished, but the depth of her relationship with God.

PART IV

Implications for a Women's Mission

We cannot flow both deep and wide.

Only God can do that.

We have only a limited number of days to live

and only a limited quantity of energy to spend.

So the important thing is to spend ourselves

as entirely as possible

upon whatever is our special calling.

AMY CARMICHAEL

Eight

Exile and Community

THERE ARE BENEFITS AND hindrances of exile in the context of birthing a new women's mission/community/order. The character and function of this particular type of community makes a clear case for new missiological thinking. These points are considered as we look at the mission community of Harvest Emergent Relief as a friaristic community with a fresh approach to leadership.

Two women's missionary movements serve as examples of how exile not only plays a part in the individual's life, but in the formation of communities. The Desert Mothers began as solitary women drawn to an exilic way of life in order to find intimacy with God, and soon others followed their example and grew into communities of sisters. Later, after the communities began to take on monastic formation, some of the women were sent out from their monasteries in order to take living water to those who were thirsty. A picture emerges and we can see the evolution of women on the mission field: from a few individual women whose hearts were set on a pilgrimage of repentance, a few seeds grew into a movement of women.

The second women's missionary movement, led in part by Helen Barrett Montgomery, determined to make a way for women sidelined and held back by their male counterparts on the foreign field. Small groups were formed as women's missions groups both sent out and financially supported women who were called to preach the good news.

Both movements began with visionary women who looked beyond their own circumstances, limitations, and setbacks. Soon others joined them as they formed bonds that grew into clusters and communities, which in time became movements. These movements were initiated in exile and carried the DNA of exile throughout their development. Without each individual embracing the primary exile, there would not have been the historical impact.

Paul Pierson reinforced this thought when he said, "So often in history, God has raised up small groups on the periphery, ignored at first, to start a new missionary effort. They have often encountered indifference and faced great odds against their projects. Perhaps they were people of no status, or their interest was directed toward neglected groups."[1] People on the periphery or the fringes have, as one would expect, known some measure of exile.

The benefits of exile are significant. First of all, learning to survive in the midst of the harsh and unrelenting desert was crucial. The physical landscape often mirrored the landscape of the soul, where life and death decisions were made. Second, clarity was gained from the choices that were made in the midst of the struggle. As priorities shifted, a new perspective on life was found. But intimacy with God was most important of all. The growth process was deep and painful, but it yielded the best fruit.

Annie Taylor's life is one example of the fruit of exile. If she had stayed in the confines of boundaried mission work in China, she would never have been able to travel to Tibet and later live on the India/Tibet border and bring others to Christ. Gladys Aylward is another example of one who set her sights on China, despite rejection from those in mission authority. By her determination to embrace the exile forced upon her, she was able to lead two hundred Chinese children over the mountains to safety as the Japanese attacked. Our final example covers the lives of Mildred Cable and the French sisters, who against all advice and warning because they were considered too old, chose to embrace exile from the missionary community in order to take the gospel to the frontiers of China. They lived in a town out on the edge and traveled to many obscure places like the Gobi desert, where Tibetan nomads roamed the country. If these women had not embraced a life of exile, those who had not heard about the God who loves would have been left without the message of hope.

These examples show the benefits of a life lived in exile, of women firmly believing that God was leading the way. Though from an earthly point of view this life may be considered too harsh and barren, from God's perspective the everlasting fruit is what mattered.

1. P. Pierson, *Dynamics of Christian Mission*, 252.

On the other hand, hindrances or detriments to the acceptance of exile in one's life can be deadly. The damages sustained because of refusal to embrace personal, physical, or spiritual exile, as from God's hand could result in defiance, bitterness, and recalcitrance, eventually leading to a hardened heart. Instead of growing closer to God, a loss of faith could occur and belief in the love of God could shrivel or even disappear. The major danger of living a solitary life of exile, if one is not hidden in God, is that of abject loneliness, disconnectedness, and unhealthy inward focus. God created us in such a way that we need communication and communion with others. The next section looks at a prototype of such a community.

Mission Community of Harvest Emergent Relief

Harvest Emergent Relief is developing into a newly formed community. It is one example of a vehicle that could lead the way for change. Women who have been outsiders, knowing some form of exile, are welcome candidates for joining HER. The goal is to develop a cohesive, coordinated unit that works in concert and coalition with other groups who have the same kingdom mindset. Hope for the future is one of the underlying components, not only for the organization, but for the members and most certainly for those we minister among.

Because HER is unique in its calling and composition, it is important for the spiritual formation to be practical. This done in the right way will help to empower and support members of HER as trust is built. Understanding the political landscape, whether it be personal or geographic, is also critical. By yoking these particular elements, building a women's mission can be done in a positive and creative way. All of this will be put into practice through leading by example in order to inspire and cultivate a healthy and radical lifestyle of friendship with Jesus.

HER is a fledging missionary order of women who are called to intimacy and action in high-risk areas of the world, including war zones. HER is a developing women's mission designed to go to limited-access countries, to the hardest places, to the dying, the hungry, and the marginalized. HER is an emerging dispersed order of women often living in precarious circumstances, but primarily focused in Asia. The HER mandate is to bring relief by rescuing the oppressed and fighting for those who have been left behind. In essence, Isaiah 58 is the mission statement and it reads in part:

> Is not this the fast which I choose;
> to loose the bonds of injustice,
> To undo the thongs of the yoke,
> to let the oppressed go free
> and break every yoke?
>
> Is it not to share your bread with the hungry
> and bring the homeless poor into your house;
> when you see the naked, to cover them;
> And not to hide yourself from your own kin?
>
> Then your light will break forth like the dawn,
> and your healing shall spring up quickly;
> your vindicator shall go before you;
> the glory of the LORD shall be your rear guard.
> (Isa 58:6–8)

Requirements for becoming a part of the HER community are seen in the following eight essentials:

1. Must adhere to the basic tenets of orthodox Christian belief.

2. Must be weak, broken, and dependent on God.

3. Must have prayer as a lifestyle.

4. Must have desire to walk with Jesus in hard places.

5. Must be willing to be misunderstood, looked at with suspicion, and rejected.

6. Must be willing to lay down life for people resistant to the gospel.

7. Must have few possessions and be willing to travel rough.

8. Must have commitment to HER as a community of sisters.

We ask for weak and broken women to join our community is because this is the protocol in scripture.

> I did not come to you with superiority of speech or of wisdom, proclaiming to you the testimony of God. For I determined to know nothing among you except Jesus Christ and Him crucified. And I was with you in weakness and in fear and in much trembling. And my message and my preaching were not in persuasive words of wisdom, but in demonstration of the Spirit and of power, that your faith should not rest on human wisdom but on the power of God. (1 Cor 2:1–5)

Because the countries or regions where we work are all limited-access and high-risk areas, women coming into HER will need to know that they are called to this kind of work. For women working on the edge and often in crisis situations, the need for appropriate plans and strategies is important.

Harnessing the power derived from the diversity of women committed to the mission is vital. Because we believe in the same goals and same God does not necessarily mean that we will agree on how to implement our shared goals. Screening of applicants is important, as each woman will be unique and not the same as the others, nor would we want her to be. Diversity brings with it a rich background of insight and wisdom, all of which we will draw upon. Miroslav Volf sums it up well by saying, "To agree on justice in conflict situations you must want more than justice; you must want embrace. There can be no justice without the will to embrace. It is, however, equally true that there can be no genuine and lasting embrace without justice."[2] This is true of those that we run to help and also those within our own community.

For Harvest Emergent Relief to be effective in its mandate, it is critical that we approach our calling as a dispersed community with humility. We must, in God's mercy, be a living example of what it means to follow Christ. The mercy we have been shown will be given to those overlooked or those in dire need due to catastrophic situations. As we live in the midst of a desperate world, we will extend the mercy of God, as well as the anchor of hope. Cornel West makes the following comment in his book Democracy Matters: "To be a Christian is to live dangerously, honestly, freely—to step in the name of love as if you may land on nothing, yet to keep stepping because the something that sustains you no empire can give you and no empire can take away."[3]

Our purpose is to free the prisoner, feed the hungry, care for the sick, cloth the naked, and rescue the ravaged. We are also called to advocacy work on behalf of those who have been forgotten. The following scripture says it well: "Speak out for those who cannot speak, for the rights of all the destitute. Speak out, judge righteously, defend the rights of the poor and needy" (Prov 31:8–9).

The heart of HER is an echo of Micah 6:8: "What does the Lord require of you? But to love mercy, do justice and walk humbly with your God."

2. Volf, Exclusion and Embrace, 216.
3. West, Democracy Matters, 172.

These foundational principles, as well as on-the-ground political savvy, will be instilled in each woman as she grows in the pioneering work of HER.

Friaristic Model

Many are crying out for a deeper life in God, a longing for authenticity in their walk with Jesus, and are looking back to the time treasured ways that followers in the early days of the church experienced. Some are being drawn to a twenty-first century monastic lifestyle, while others are compelled to live out more of a missional emphasis with a "friaristic" expression. Friaristic is a term that is often associated with Saint Francis of Assisi. He and his merry band of followers took Jesus at his word and embraced a lifestyle of poverty and suffering in order to preach the good news to all who would listen. Not well known is that Saint Clare, also of Assisi, sent out sisters to take aid to those in need. They were uncompromising in their resolve to care for the poor and preach the good news of salvation. And in so doing, many of the women were martyred, but they considered it a privilege to lay down their lives in friendship with God.

One of the most compelling friaristic models is that of a dispersed order. I am defining a dispersed order as a community of believers who take vows and are bonded together, though living in different geographical locations. One of the bonding ways of our order/community can be praying the Divine Office (Liturgy of the Hours), a way of prayer used in ancient times by early church monastics, in rhythm with one another. Another way is in coming together at different times from different countries into one place in order to worship, wait on the Lord, pray, and strategize.

Jesus's words from the Sermon on the Mount not only give us instruction but pause as we reflect on what God has called us to do. Longing to be humble and merciful and hungry for the things of God, to be pure in heart and peacemakers in the midst of wars in our world and in our hearts, these are worthy goals for Jesus's followers.

Today the place of our calling may be slightly different than that of Saint Francis and Saint Clare but the fundamentals are the same: that of moving in the love and prophetic heart of God. Our mission is to relieve suffering by going with a heart grounded in prayer. Above all, we are to lift the cross of Christ so that others may see and feel the hands and feet of Jesus. A friaristic order that is dependent on the nurture of God as its primary ingredient is best suited to meet the needs and callings of today.

Elton Trueblood, in his book *The Yoke of Christ and Other Sermons,* has some interesting things to say regarding an "order." He says, "The idea that is developing so powerfully is the idea of an order. An order is a society of persons, united by some common rule of obligation. The reformation that is sought is that by which the church as we know it becomes an order in this sense."[4]

Trueblood goes on to say, "We shall not get very far until we establish, within each church, a hard core of men and women who have sufficient toughness to put the promotion of the Christian cause first in their lives."[5] Today the face of the church is changing. No longer will the church be able to go about "business" as usual, because the world needs to see an authentic faith. Trueblood says, "In any event, we shall not bring back the Christian vitality we need until we have groups who follow a discipline of time so clear that they give unhesitating priority for the Christian obligation."[6]

One example of an order that a woman created occurred in the early 1900s. God led Amy Carmichael to rescue babies offered to idols in the brothels of South India and she named her community Dohnavur Fellowship.

Dohnavur Fellowship had many facets of life and ministry, but at one point desired a fresh expression of their community. A few of the young women came to Carmichael and wanted to unite in an act of deeper consecration. Eventually a community was formed within a community, when they took vows and offered themselves to the Lord alone for his work and his good pleasure. They studied together the writings of the old mystics; they prayed together, lived in community, forged deep friendships, and waited on the Lord collectively. They served as the Lord did, with great humility.

This band of sisters came to be known as the "Sisters of the Common Life," a small group of Indian women brought together by their desire to walk closely with their Savior.[7] These women knew the cost of exile, even in their own country. Most of them had been rescued from sexual and physical abuse. Some were abandoned by their families and left to die. A form of exile was forced upon them; it was not chosen. But because of this, they were rescued and embraced by a community.

---

4. Trueblood, *Yoke of Christ*, 120.

5. Ibid., 125.

6. Ibid.

7. Houghton, *Amy Carmichael of Dohnavur*, 217.

"'*The Cross is the attraction.*' This was one of our words from the first," writes Carmichael. "For the symbol of the Church is not a burning bush nor a dove, nor an open book, nor a halo round a submissive head, nor a crown of splendid honor. It is a Cross."[8] After much prayer, the band of sisters wrote down a confession—their vows—and each woman signed it. These vows were taken for life. (For more information see appendix C, Amy Carmichael: Sisters of the Common Life.)

Choosing to come out of forced exile, many women continued to join the Sisters of the Common Life and embraced a full and devoted life to the Lover of their souls. The choice of exile unto God often brings with it a deeper walk. This could be a true model for HER to ponder as lives are brought together. Carmichael quoted Lilias Trotter (from her private diary) as to the kind of people that God gives power:

> So many questions lie ahead concerning the work, and a great comforting came this morning in the chapter of Job (Job 28) about "the way" of wisdom and "the place thereof" (verse 23). It tells how God finds the way for the wind and the water and the lightning, and it came with a blessed power what those ways are. The way for the wind is the region of the greatest emptiness, the way for the water is to the place of the lowest depth, the way for the lightning, as science proves, is along the line of the greatest weakness.[9]

This is a picture of exile and truly a picture of God's ways.

Carmichael added, "We profess to be strangers and pilgrims, seeking after a country of our own, yet we settle down in the most un-stranger-like fashion, exactly as if we were quite at home and meant to stay as long as we could. I don't wonder apostolic miracles have died. Apostolic living certainly has."[10] We are to be a people of exile, led by the Holy Spirit, doing the works of Jesus.

Another order of women to consider in this regard is Mother Teresa's "Sisters of Charity" with its main house located in Calcutta, India. Much is known about her life and the nuns who worked alongside her, so I will not add a good deal more. But I did discover that Mother Teresa also knew a form of exile as she went through her own dark night of the soul, which lasted for many years. Her personal perseverance in the face of not knowing the presence of God but instead trusting in the promises throughout this

---

8. Carmichael, *Gold Cord*, 161; italics in the original.

9. Ibid., 92.

10. Houghton, *Amy Carmichael of Dohnavur*, 88.

darkness is something to hold close. During this time when the darkness was especially intense, she said, "I have loved Him blindly, totally, only. I use every power in me—in spite of my feelings to make Him loved personally by the Sisters and the people. I will let Him have a free Hand with and in me."[11]

She was tested in her faith and yet she continued to love the very least of the least among the poor. The inner vow of her life was "Don't look for big things, just do small things with great love . . . The smaller the thing, the greater must be our love."[12] The spiritual stamina exhibited by Mother Teresa and her sisters is a large element of the faith that can drive all of us into the hard places of ministry.

Revisioning Leadership

Attention to the best style of leadership is critical in the process of creating a new mission. Marguerite Shuster explains that the task of a leader is to define reality, but it must be done with the grounded acceptance of our own finitude, as well as our own sinfulness, bathed in grace. Shuster says,

> In the end, then, no theological principle is more central than our human need for grace—God's saving grace first of all, but secondarily those manifestations of grace potentially reflected in every aspect of our daily lives. Only by keeping a firm grasp on grace can leaders even risk seeing accurately themselves and others, in all their potential and in all their frailty; for only thus are there resources for dealing with the surprising capacities and the surprising faults that can both appear as threats. And leaders who know deeply their own need for grace, who grant grace to others, and who seek forthrightly to do what they do before God, are in the best position to view reality—even before they seek to define it—in a way that honors the Lord.[13]

Wilbert R. Shenk underscores the foundation of Christian leadership when he says, "In the body of Christ, leaders should understand their primary role as cooperating with God."[14] Above all, a leader must be one who follows hard after Christ, extends mercy without end, moves in gratitude

11. Mother Teresa and Kolodiejchuk, *Mother Teresa*, 185.

12. Ibid., 34.

13. Shuster, "Leadership as Interpreting Reality," 23.

14. Shenk, "Paying Attention to People," 179.

without measure, and empowers with true humility. A leader brings energy and vision to the table, but especially seeks to cooperate with all that God has purposed. When one aligns with God's purposes, everything else flows naturally/supernaturally. This is truly the task of the leader: to know intimacy with God, being led by the Spirit and walking in faithful friendship with Jesus.

When confronting gender bias in leadership, the painful truth is that it can still be found in the church, the missionary community, and the world at large. Caroline Sweetman gets right to the point in her book *Women and Leadership*, as she makes the following statement: "If leadership is male-dominated, gender biases in distribution and control of resources will remain, and women will continue to be more vulnerable to economic poverty and social marginalization."[15] Laboring to end gender bias in leadership is at the heart of the struggle for many in the missionary world.

We cannot expect to bring change to oppressed countries where women are still seen as male property, if we will not deal with it first of all in the body of Christ. If the missionary world continues to practice the same model of leadership in their church-planting endeavors, they will continue to not only have women not in leadership, but will keep women in bondage as well. We must help to chart a course for women not only in the Western world, but in countries where women have no freedom at all.

HER wants to attract the kind of women who have the following qualities: women who have been outsiders, who place a high value on relationships and direct communication; women who want to lead from the center and are leery of hierarchies; and women who want to see the big picture. All of these women have known some measure of exile and, because of that, these qualities are evident. Only good followers make good leaders.

Practical Application: High-Risk Areas

The rogue and oppressive nations of Asia, and in particular Southeast Asia, are one of HER's main focal points for ministry. This region is riddled with corruption, rogue governments, poverty, and oppression of all kinds: human trafficking; children trained to become soldiers; forced prostitution; methamphetamine laboratories on the borders; refugees; AIDS victims; rape; women and children used as landmine sweepers; and the list goes on. It is one of many areas in the world that is in desperate need of justice

15. Sweetman, *Women and Leadership*, 3.

intervention. Millions of people live under the oppressive hand of military dictatorships. Many people in these places remain in forced exile within their own country. Thousands more refugees have escaped to the borders or into other countries and now live in exile.

The borderlands of specific nations are examples of places where indigenous women are trying to bring about change for their country and themselves. The women of the majority people as well as all ethnic groups are oppressed within and without their country. Women are treated as convenient, usable, and disposable property. A man overheard talking about women in Burma stated that after centuries of following their men, women now walk ahead. The women are now forced to walk ahead because there are still many unexploded land mines due to the ongoing war and the men do not want to die!

Monique Skidmore and Patricia Lawrence write about their research in *Women and the Contested State*, saying, "Case studies presented here show small spaces for community networking and the fostering of solidarity in conflict zones by women. Women's agency is made manifest in the creation of these networks during crisis periods and their continuation in the aftermath."[16]

Women are trying to build a new way of life for their people on many borders within Asia. Strong ethnic women are an example of those organizing to overcome the degradation that forced them into physical and emotional exile. In the small wedge of territory known as the borderland, there is a great opportunity for fighting injustice alongside these women. Together we can focus on stopping the inhumanity of brutal armies towards women as they use rape as a weapon of war. The women of HER would be uniquely qualified to not only stand with these women leaders, but to show them the mercy and love of Jesus.

In her paper, "Borderlands and Women," Mary O'Kane says,

> Women activists displaced from Burma and without formal or effective state protection are rendered effectively stateless, suspended in a legal limbo in the Burma-Thailand borderlands. Despite this entrapment, the borderlands provide opportunities for women's collective action not possible elsewhere: neither within Burma nor Thailand, nor in other countries where women activists from Burma may be dispersed.[17]

16. Skidmore and Lawrence, *Women and the Contested State*, 5–6.
17. O'Kane, "Borderlands and Women," 1.

O'Kane discusses the word "refugee" used by those who are now outside of Burma. She spoke with one woman who said, "Actually, in my mind, refugee is not a good word . . . We are exiled people. We just want to say that we are exiles who believe in our opinions and democratic vision."[18] The topic of exile surfaces constantly when confronted with injustice, as does the problem of gender bias.

On the borders of select countries, there are distinct possibilities of working to bring justice in the areas of child soldier rescue, prostitution, those with leprosy, those dying of AIDS, and refugees fleeing to what they believe is safety. The area is a hotbed of activity as different ethnic armies are often not only struggling with each other but also fighting to stay alive while the government army plunders the villages and ravages the people. Ethnic armies fight against one another but they are all somewhat united in their struggle against the enemy.

The overlapping praxis on the borders shows itself uniquely in that feminists from the West are helping a few women's groups, and a women's mission could bring the power and presence of Jesus to bear in their struggle for justice. Women who are Christians and have the experience of knowing exile from the larger Christian world are uniquely qualified to bring depth as well as action. My research demonstrates that the more intensely exile was experienced, the more challenging the work God called the women to do. As noted earlier, the historical pioneering women who knew exile are tremendous examples of this.

As we move across borders and boundaries and lands left desolate by conflict and pain, we must remember that the "Cross is the attraction." The cross is always what we must lift up and bring to our friends who are suffering on the borderlands and also in our midst. Knowing that Jesus suffered the deepest exile will strengthen our hearts as we are bound together.

18. Ibid., 3.

NINE

A New Women's Missionary Movement

THE CREATION OF A pioneering women's mission such as HER could have a catalytic effect, enabling the emergence of a new movement. Women of exile formed into a mission of their own would have questioned traditional missionary approaches and taken the risk to trust God in new and demanding situations. This, in part, clears the way for a movement. Dana Robert, missiologist, says, "The time has come for a new vision of the role of women in the mission of the church."[1] Finding the right women and clearly defining the goals will bring about needed change. It is not a matter of repackaging or revising, but of recovering the truth of women standing in the forefront of radical activity and the frontiers of faith for God's kingdom.

A fresh understanding of what it means for a mission to multiply is expressed through the growth of a women's movement. In the section on social movement theory, I discussed the difference between consensus and conflict movements. The nature of what God has called us to do can be found in the perspectives of both insiders and outsiders. The insiders have a distinct position from which to critique the decisions and indeed the history of what makes up the present-day missionary world. Outsiders have the unique opportunity to introduce fresh insight and vision as we take on the challenges of the twenty-first century. A women's movement made up of communities has the capacity to bring those who have been exiled into

1. Robert, "Revisioning the Women's Missionary Movement," 112.

a new calling from God. An exile community is a definition of what some would call a default culture.[2]

Developing a New Default Culture

A women's missionary movement could in reality be the development of a new default culture, a movement made up of different orders or communities, each of which began through the vision of a single individual, and joined together with others in a common goal. Different expressions of the movement will all have one thing in common: a covenantal community based on trust. This default culture, this covenantal community, will consist of women with a new identity who have been called to engage in a fresh expression of the call to ministry. There is much to learn about how to bring together a marginalized group of Jesus followers and form them into a real community of trust, but one thing is certain: it will consist of women who know the mercy of God and want to extend that to others.

Of course the foundation of this monastic-missionary movement is the true worship and praise of God. "At the heart of the gospel is a confidence that praise of God is a real possibility even from the depths of human existence. Moreover, it is a praise that is focused on Christ and buoyed along in the same Spirit that raised Jesus from the dead."[3] Mark Labberton says in his book *The Dangerous Act of Worship*, "Worship does not remove us from exile, but it shapes how we live there."[4] A community that has embraced its status of exile can relate well to a people who have been driven from their own country or those who have been shunned from society because of disease and disdain.

Each community or "order of friends" must first of all vow to keep Jesus Christ as the core of their life together and ultimately the movement. In actuality, this is not a new idea but a return not only to scripture, which speaks of a "house of friends" (Jer 13:6), but also to the "old ways" that were practiced beginning with the early church. This passage speaks of being "wounded in the house of my friends," but a new order of friends will be a place of healing. What was once an individual's life of exile, can be turned

2. The phrase "default culture" was borrowed from Sherwood G. Lingenfelter, *Leading Cross-Culturally*, 71–72.

3. Pickard, *Liberating Evangelism*, 98.

4. Labberton, *Dangerous Act of Worship*, 146.

into a place of resolve as women band together to walk in a corporate exile of God's choosing.

Much of the missionary world is organized toward task orientation. The development of new women's communities changes the trajectory to have a relational base, just as Jesus did in his ministry. Recapturing the essence of that life will once again bring an authentic voice to what is truly the good news, and has the potential to be the reality without the rhetoric, nuance without numbers, and kindness without calculation.

"Early Christianity seems to have been exciting partly because the new members lived dangerously. God might lead them any day to pull up stakes and go far away to try to start a new chapter of the sacred Order."[5] There was nothing safe or comfortable about following Jesus in the beginning. Only after Constantine did the life of a Christian become risk free. But it was then, when life became unbearably easy that a few determined women and men fled to the desert to find real encounter with Christ. The culture they developed brought hungry seekers from the towns out into the desert to find these sisters and brothers in order to gain wisdom.

As discussed earlier, there has been much misunderstanding about the role of these lovers of Jesus who forsook everything in order to be found by God. But the historical records of the Desert Mothers are calling out to be reconsidered at this point in time. Communities/friaristic orders are places where women can find the longing that God has put within them, which is to create a new culture. Establishing a default culture will bring women who have known exile into fulfilling their part of the great ingathering.

People will come against this order of women, this community of friends, this movement but what does that matter? They came against Jesus, and he promises persecution for all who follow after him. Maybe it is time for a theology of suffering to give birth to a spirit of martyrdom that will emerge in this postmodern culture. Maybe when we begin to take our faith seriously, then those who are not yet believers may be drawn, yes, compelled to investigate what they see.

5. Trueblood, *Yoke of Christ*, 123.

Momentum

Southern Methodist missionary Nannie Gaines said, "No country can rise higher than her women."[6] Those words alone are a rallying cry and a call for the missiology of women to be more deeply developed.

Dana Robert makes the following comment: "Although the needs and opportunities seem ripe for a new women's missionary movement, involvement of women in mission today must differ from the earlier women's movement in certain key respects. The most important change from the earlier women's mission movement is that paternalism must be left in the past."[7] She then goes on to state three more changes that must take place: (1) the consequences of always contextualizing women's issues; (2) the significance of deeper conversion; and (3) the unleashing of the Holy Spirit.[8]

Mission organizations frequently use the phrase that they are being "culturally appropriate" to mask the continuing oppression of women. "But if the goal of a women's missionary movement is spiritual and physical 'liberation' then how does a women's movement grapple with cultural indigenization that may in fact leave women in the same oppressive social situation as before they were Christians?" Robert ends with this question: "When the Holy Spirit saves women's souls and frees their spirits, is it not an act of faithlessness when the mission of the church ignores their oppression in the name of contextualization?"[9] My belief is that the issue of "contextualization" in missionary work has been taken too far. Yes, one must deeply be a part of the culture, but it is important to remember that all culture is fallen. "Contextualization" is often used not only to mask the continued oppression of women but it also allows a syncretism of belief systems. When this happens, the veracity of the gospel is subverted and the truth of who Jesus really is becomes diluted, until there is nothing left but a murky mixture of unbelief.

The momentum for a movement begins and continues by the work of the Holy Spirit. Without the Spirit, who leads us into all truth, there is no guidance, no power, and no lasting fruit. Therefore intimacy with the Holy Spirit is paramount. The Spirit always points us to Jesus. And after we come

---

6. Robert, *American Women in Mission*, 411.

7. Robert, "Revisioning the Women's Missionary Movement," 115.

8. Ibid., 115–16.

9. Ibid., 117.

to Jesus, real friendship begins. Without becoming friends with God, we will have no true basis for friendship with others.

Summary

The goal of building a women's mission is shown in the following ways: (1) women who have been sidelined for whatever reason will now have a place from which to minister; (2) women will be able to engage other women in countries where there is very little or nonexistent freedom for women; (3) women will be able to accept a radical call to stand up and follow Jesus into the physically and spiritually dark places of different societies where unspeakable acts are being committed; (4) women will be able to bring the freedom of Christ to bear by bringing justice to those who have been severely abused and broken by unjust governments and societal systems; and (5) following the leading of the Holy Spirit, women will be able to build communities of trust that will enable growth by giving sanctuary to those women on the run in various countries.

Hopefully, this gives the reader a deeper understanding of how a mission that is made up of many who have been exiled and marginalized in their own lives, will be able to minister to those who are experiencing exile themselves.

Ten

Conclusion

THE SACRED PLACE OF Exile: Pioneering Women and the Need for a New Women's Missionary Movement is a response to the hidden cry of those who are outsiders. My hope is that a new hermeneutic has been uncovered which will help to bridge the gap between the old way of traditional mission protocol and a new way of utilizing the gifts and the callings of women who are marginalized and who live in exile.

Two outcomes of the study are clear:

- In order for change to take place in our missiological thinking, there is need for a new way of seeing what is lacking in our missionary mandate.

- Women who are outsiders need to have the opportunity to find their place with other pioneering women who have known some measure of exile.

My research has shown that life-defining moments varied for the women studied, but all had an unmistakable call from God to go beyond traditional missionary standards. The conversion experiences played a significant role in the choices they made. In addition, the focus on women missionary mentors revealed the galvanizing effect that exile had on their lives. It was also clear that a life lived in exile is often leveraged by God and used as a prophetic statement/witness/lifestyle. Often, the women made deliberate decisions to be involved in justice issues as part of their ministry. Using these women's lives, experiences, and needs as a backdrop, a strong case can be made for the creation of a women's mission that is friaristic in nature, with a monastic-missionary flavor for the spreading of the gospel.

History tells us that once major societal change, revolutionary movements, or personal transformations have taken place the next generation of believers often takes a step back. What was once radical slowly steers itself into the mainstream and deep discipleship fades away. Once again those who have settled for the status quo and a comfortable existence begin to quash those who have become the disconnected and the disenfranchised of the day.

Jim Wallis, in his *Agenda for Biblical People*, makes this statement:

> The gospel presented in the New Testament is a scandal to the values and standards of the world, whose condition is dominated by the cycle of death. Although assimilations, complicity and compromise best describe the modern church's relationship to the world, the gospel is in direct collision with the world system. Talk of realism, respectability and reasonableness dominates the conversations of contemporary religion, but the New Testament speaks of the abandonment, insecurity, persecution and exile that come from seeking first the kingdom. A church of comfort, property, privilege and position stands in sharp contrast with the biblical description of the people of God as aliens, exiles, sojourners, strangers and pilgrims.[1]

As believers, our own exile from God is no longer in question. We are welcomed as children into the kingdom of God. But for the sake of those who do not know God, we must take up the mantle of exile and go to those on the outside. My proposal for a new women's mission made up of those who have not found a place in either the institutional church or traditional mission organizations will hopefully find a way to follow Jesus in an authentic and truthful way.

Many people ask, "Why should we have a woman-only mission?" and my reply is always definite. As leaders we must make a place for those who have not been heard. Women bring a special ingredient into the mix when we live out the kingdom of God among those who are marginalized and outside the gates. To my knowledge, there is no such entity in the evangelical missionary world known as a "women's mission" working in high-risk areas. A century ago, there were quite a few, but they died off as men became involved and took over the leadership. The desert mother movement of the

---

1. Wallis, *Agenda for Biblical People*, 2.

fourth century and the women's missionary movement of the nineteenth century set a precedent for a new women's mission and movement to come forth, and the time has come to once and for all capitalize on these initial efforts.

The challenges that have dealt near mortal blows to the women missionaries who have not fit the norm have left them scattered as afterthoughts throughout the pages of history. To bring together remnants of hopes and dreams of these women into a community setting is worthy of God's call. As we build alliances and collaborate with one another and others of like mind, God's purposes will be accomplished, because we have been given specific works to do and places to be and people to love. Given that belief, we can bless one another to walk in whatever the calling is upon our lives, without bias or belligerence.

Injustice in its many forms is a call to believing women, not only to fight for our own rights, but also to fight for those who literally cannot fight for themselves. Those who choose to embrace the "foolishness of the cross" and a lifestyle lived "outside the camp" will make a way for injustice to be uprooted. "In the final analysis, the only available options are either to reject the Cross and with it the core of the Christian faith or to take up one's cross and follow the Crucified—and be scandalized ever anew by the challenge."[2] The Apostle Paul said, "For I determined to know nothing among you except Jesus Christ and him crucified" (1 Cor 2:2 NASV).

My intention has been to cast a vision and show why the times in which we live cry out for a new way of approaching missions. I have explained why radicalized women who come from outside the church, as well as outside the missionary community are ready to take their place not only in the *missio Dei* but also in the *missio Spiritus*, the mission of the Spirit. Hopefully, a wide net has been cast so that those who are willing to embrace the calling of God will have others who will walk with them in radical discipleship, remembering that today's harvest field will be tomorrow's frontline messengers of the gospel of Jesus.

2. Volf, *Exclusion and Embrace*, 26.

Appendix A

Interview Question Categories: Contemporary Women Missionaries

- Family life
- Spiritual awareness
- Social/political consciousness
- Friendship/ mentoring
- Crucible
- Exile

Appendix B

Early Women's Missions

1800 — Boston Female Society for Missionary Purposes (Baptist and Congregational)

1801 — Boston Female Society for the Promotion and Diffusion of Christian Knowledge. (Congregational)

1803 — Female Missionary Society of Southampton, Mass. (Congregational)

1808 — Female Mite Society of Beverly, Mass. (Baptist)

1811 — Salem Female Cent Society, Massachusetts. (Baptist)

1812 — Female Foreign Missionary Society of New Haven, Conn. (Congregational)

1814 — Fayette Street Church Women's Missionary Society. (Baptist)

1816 — Female Charitable Society of Tallmadge, Ohio. (Congregational) (Sent first contribution received from west of the Alleghenies by the American Board)

1819 — Wesleyan Seminary Missionary Society (Methodist)

1823 — Society for the Support of Heathen (Presbyterian)

1835 — Society for the Evangelization of the World, Newark, NJ (Presbyterian)

1847 — Free Baptist Female Missionary Society, Sutton, VT. Never disbanded.

1848 — Ladies China Missionary Society, Baltimore. (Methodist)[1]

---

1. Montgomery, *Western Women in Eastern Lands*, 19.

Requirements of Historic Mission Groups

Annie Taylor: Tibet Pioneer Mission

THE FOLLOWING ARE THE principles, doctrine, and requirements for any wishing to join the Tibet Pioneer Mission. I quote at length in order for the reader to take in the full flavor of what Taylor is saying.[1]

> The object of the mission is to evangelize Tibet, and so remove one of the last barriers to the fulfillment of our Lord's words, 'This Gospel of the Kingdom shall be preached in all the world for a witness unto all nations; and then the end shall come.' The principles upon which the Mission is worked are those of the China Inland Mission. But the main object of the Mission being to afford every Tibetan the opportunity of hearing the Gospel, it is purposed that the work of the Mission will be pioneering until such time as this object is accomplished.

> True-hearted and humble-minded men and women of God, full of the Holy Ghost and faith, experienced in Gospel work, and who have been used of God in winning souls and holding the doctrines mentioned below, will be eligible as candidates, irrespective of what branch of the Church of Christ they belong to.

> The Mission is supported entirely by the freewill offerings of the Lord's people. The needs of the work are laid before God in prayer, no personal solicitations or collections being authorized. No more is expended than is thus received, going into debt being

1. Broomhall, *Last Letters*, 75—77.

inconsistent with the principle of entire dependence upon God. The director therefore cannot, and does not promise or guarantee any fixed amount of support to the workers. She seeks faithfully to distribute the funds available, and to meet the need of each worker; but they are expected to recognize that their dependence for the supply of their need is on God, who called them, and for whom they have gone to labour, and not on the human organization.

It will be required that those who seek to join the Mission be sound in the faith on all the main points of Christian doctrine, which may be particularized as follows:

> The divine inspiration of the Scriptures;
> The Trinity of the Godhead;
> The fall of man and his consequent need of regeneration;
> The atonement for man's sin;
> Justification by faith in Christ alone;
> The resurrection of the dead;
> The eternity of reward and punishment.

They will also be asked to give their personal experience of the guidance of the Holy Spirit and the efficacy of prayer, as being points of importance to the life of the missionary.

Candidates for the Mission are requested to communicate with Miss Taylor.

Amy Carmichael: Sisters of the Common Life

My Vow:
Whatsoever Thou sayest unto me, by Thy grace, I will do it.
My Constraint:
Thy love, O Christ, my Lord.
My Confidence:
Thou art able to keep that which I have committed unto Thee.
My Joy:
To do Thy will, O God.
My Discipline:
That which I would not choose, but that which Thy love appoints.
My Prayer:
Conform my will to Thine.
My Motto:
Love to live, Live to love.
My Portion:
The Lord is the portion of mine inheritance.

Teach us, good Lord, to serve Thee more faithfully; to give and not to count the cost; to fight and not to heed the wounds; to toil and not to seek for rest; to labor and not to seek for any reward, save that of knowing that we do Thy will, O Lord our God.[2]

2. Carmichael, *Gold Cord*, 178—79.

Appendix C

Hudson Taylor: Core Values of the China Inland Mission

Object. The China Inland Mission was formed under a deep sense of China's pressing need, and with an earnest desire, constrained by the love of CHRIST and the hope of His coming, to obey His command to preach the Gospel to every creature. Its aim is, by the help of GOD, to bring the Chinese to a saving knowledge of the love of GOD in CHRIST, by means of itinerant and localised work throughout the whole of the interior of China.

Character. The Mission is Evangelical, and embraces members of all the leading denominations of Christians.

Methods. Methods somewhat unusual and peculiar were adopted for working the newly-proposed organisation. It was determined:

1. That duly qualified candidates for missionary labour should be accepted without restriction as to denomination, provided there was soundness in the faith in all fundamental truths.

2. That all who went out as Missionaries should go in dependence upon God for temporal supplies, with the clear understanding that the Mission did not guarantee any income whatever; and knowing that, as the Mission would not go into debt, it could only minister to those connected with it as the funds sent in from time to time might allow.

Support. The Mission is supported entirely by the free-will offerings of the Lord's people. The needs of the work are laid before God in prayer, no personal solicitations or collections being authorised. No more is expended than is thus received, going into debt being considered inconsistent with the principle of entire dependence upon God.[3]

3. Broomall, *Last Letters*, appendix.

Appendix D

Unique Requirements for Harvest Emergent Relief

THE REQUIREMENTS FOR BECOMING a part of the Harvest Emergent Relief community are seen in the following eight essentials.

1. Must adhere to the basic tenets of orthodox Christian belief.

2. Must be weak, broken, and dependent on God.

3. Must have fasting and prayer as a lifestyle.

4. Must have desire to walk with Jesus in hard places.

5. Must be willing to be misunderstood, looked at with suspicion, and rejected.

6. Must be willing to lay down life for people resistant to the gospel.

7. Must have few possessions and be willing to travel rough.

8. Must have commitment to HER as a community of sisters.

Appendix E

Fledgling Plan

A BASIC PLAN FOR the women's mission Harvest Emergent Relief includes these specific areas: (1) our life together; (2) our life dispersed; and (3) our life on specific missions.

Our life together will necessitate a kind of mother-house where all can come to be renewed and refreshed, a point of stability that is a haven and a refuge.

Our life dispersed will involve communication that keeps our sisters in the same rhythm of life no matter where they are located.

Our life on specific missions in specific danger/war zones is more complicated. I foresee a structure that is a mission unit. The success of the unit in every situation will depend on the ability to move both vertically and horizontally. The whole group will discuss decisions and strategies, but execution and implementation, by necessity, will be different. Leadership structure will change depending on where we are. Specific leaders will be in charge when the actions are to take place. Each person will have assigned tasks and duties that are to be done quickly. If it is a life and death situation, then precision will be mandatory.

Given the nature of the work, we can worship, wait on God, pray together, intercede, discuss vigorously, and strategize. Each woman will have input, share insight, and lend her voice. Once we have made the plans, we can move as a unit with one person in charge for the specific mission at the time.

Appendix F

One Woman's Sojourn: A Story of Lament

NOT TOO LONG AGO, I had a friend who was called to preach the gospel in the hardest places, in the regions where people had not heard the message of Messiah Yeshua/Jesus. And so she went, leaving behind all that would compete with allegiance to her Redeemer. She climbed the high places of Tibet as well as the high places of her heart. Finally, after almost twenty years she led a young Tibetan lad to the foot of the cross and into the kingdom of God. She rejoiced for this and shed tears of great delight! At last, fruit!

This was no small thing and yet a heavy lament hung inside her. She asked God, herself, and others many questions, among them, the timing of the Tibetan people to come to God, the identification of strongholds that held them back from seeing the light, the equipping of the missionaries that have gone before, the hardness of the Tibetan heart, and so on.

She identified with Job, not in his righteousness and reverence, but in his solitude and the stripping of sane thoughts, as she struggled to find answers to the interminable questions that plagued her soul. Aside from those necessary queries, a cry remained within her heart and a raging ache that heaved up a mostly silent throbbing wonder.

The darkness came and she could not comprehend what had happened. The presence of God that had always guided her was missing. She could not find him in the darkness. Whether it was spiritual darkness from the powers around her or a spiritual darkness of her own making, still she sought him whom her soul loved. Job's thoughts were in her ears:

"Oh that I knew where I might find Him, that I might come to His seat" (Job 23:3 NASB).

Had she compromised somewhere along the way? Did her past make her unfit for the work? She had fallen again, did that disqualify her? Were her broken parts too broken? Job's wail broke through her own sobs, "My spirit is broken, my days are extinguished, the grave is ready for me" (Job 17:1 NASB).

She had known many years of friendship with God. Job had known friendship for years as well. Was a close relationship with God now completely out of reach? It all seemed over; it seemed to be only a grinding memory.

> Oh, that I were as in months gone by,
> As in the days when God watched over me;
> When His lamp shone over my head,
> And by His light I walked through darkness;
> As I was in the prime of my days,
> When the friendship of God was over my tent . . .
> (Job 29:2—4 NASB)

She thought back over the years . . . not welcomed by standard mission agencies, this missionary friend of mine felt shunned. She asked questions: Is there no justice? What have I done? Is there no one to fight for me, to plead my cause? I feel outside the camp, banished and exiled! Is there no one to intervene? "There is no umpire between us, who may lay his hand upon us both" (Job 9:33 NASB).

She cried out to God who had promised there would be those who labored with her; there would be fellowship of the deepest kind in the journey. She had always walked apart; she was solitary and lonely. Was there fairness?

Was this truly her calling or had she been duped by her own sense of adventure? She scraped her soul with caustic questions, like Job had scraped his flesh with a potsherd. Maybe she had never known him. She could echo Job's refrain:

> Were He to pass by me, I would not see Him;
> Were He to move past me, I would not perceive Him.
> Were He to snatch away, who could restrain Him?
> Who could say to Him, "What are You doing?"
> (Job 9:11—12 NASB)

Though she no longer wanted to live, she determined not to complain, mostly because she was afraid of the same acrimony of soul that had come upon Job. "I loathe my own life; I will speak in the bitterness of my soul" (Job 10:1 NASB). Still her lament continued in an unbroken litany of wail upon wail. Her desperate cry of feeling forsaken and alone could not be contained. It was consuming her. She would mumble in her wine, "If you will not use me, then why don't you just take my life?" Would this exile tear apart her soul? Her heart again resonated with the words of Job:

> Why then have you brought me out of the womb?
> Would that I had died and no eye had seen me!
> I should have been as though I had not been . . .
> (Job 10:18—19 NASB)

The questions seemed to mount with wings like vultures and throw her to the ground. Who could deliver her?

As she spoke the next words, her countenance changed. She said that the answers seemed to tumble down from above. Jesus seemed to answer both Job and the missionary. Looking with great love in his eyes, he said,

> Have I been so long with you and yet you have not come to know Me.
> (John 14:9 NASB)

Jesus spoke of friendship and intimacy. He said they were no longer slaves or strangers but God's friends; to prove his love he had laid down his life. And as for feeling "outside the camp," banished and exiled, his life spoke what needed to be said. Jesus told the missionary to remember her prayers to him. She had asked to be like him, to walk with him and be able to speak to the Tibetan people in ways they could understand. They were a people of exile, banished from their home. They lived far outside the camp!

Jesus reminded her that he has always chosen the weak and the weary, the broken and the disgruntled. Paul even chimed in with words:

> But God has chosen the foolish things of the world to shame the wise, and God has chosen the weak things of the world to shame the things that are strong, and the base things of the world and the despised, God has chosen the things that are not that He might nullify the things that are, that no one should boast before God.
> (1 Cor 1:27—29 NASB)

God speaks to them from the sermon Jesus gave on the mountain: Blessed are the poor in spirit and those who mourn. Blessed are the gentle and those who hunger and thirst for righteousness. Blessed are the merciful and the pure in heart and the peacemakers. Blessed are those who have been persecuted for the sake of righteousness; and don't forget that you are blessed when people throw insults at you (Matt 5:3—11).

Jesus reminds Job and the lamenting missionary who lives in exile that the symbols of the kingdom of God can be found in service, suffering, and dying. The missionary had heard someone speak of this before, but now the words from her notebook took a dramatic turn and she realized that the choices must be made in the grit of it all, once again.

As she wondered how much of this cup she must drink, her thoughts were interrupted before they were finished. She heard the words of Jesus in her heart, "To drink the cup is to stay yoked to Me." She knew the cup of suffering was filled with many things; one of them was choosing to suffer with the suffering of others. But the deepest suffering comes when the opposition of your own heart rages and yet you still decide not to turn back. The choice is exile.

Turning the corner, crawling across the line, she fell into a heap, choosing to believe that God is true and there is no one else. She conceded that the world was bigger than her own pain and that the selfishness of her own misery must yield to God's plan of the ages. God has created a moral universe and there is such a thing as cause and effect; the choices we make have consequences even in the unseen realm. When the final curtain is thrown back for all time, for all to see, then we will know. When the last bit of the tapestry of history has been woven and all we can see is the ugliness of our own lives, then our great God will flip it over and the beauty will finally be seen. The lamenting missionary was finally able to join Job's chorus:

> But He knows the way that I take. When He has tried me, I shall come forth as gold. . . . For He performs what is appointed for me. (Job 23:10, 14 NASB)

As she embraced the words of Job in her own heart, she began to hear faint whispers of her Beloved. It was the voice of the One who called her to run with him on the mountains. Her Beloved had called her to himself! Jesus was the one she would labor with on the high places of Tibet and wherever else they would run together. It all made more sense to her and yet there still remained the gray, clouded, constant pain within her own heart as she wrestled with the shadows over Tibet.

The story goes on, but she said that was enough for now. How does one explain the exile that is chosen for another?

Bibliography

Afkhami, Mahnaz. *Women In Exile.* Charlottesville, VA: University Press of Virginia, 1994.

Anderson, Fil. *Breaking the Rules: Trading Performance for Intimacy with God.* Downers Grove, IL: InterVarsity Press, 2010.

Anderson, Gerald H., ed. *Biographical Dictionary of Christian Missions.* New York: Macmillan, 1998.

———. *Mission Legacies: Biographical Studies of the Modern Missionary Movement.* Maryknoll, NY: Orbis Books, 1994.

Aptheker, Bettina F. *Intimate Politics: How I Grew Up Red, Fought for Free Speech and Became A Feminist Rebel.* Emeryville, CA: Seal Press, 2006.

Archer, Margaret S. *Being Human: The Problem of Agency.* Cambridge: Cambridge University Press, 2000.

Baker, H. A. *Visions Beyond the Veil.* Springdale, PA: Whitaker House, 1973.

Baker, Heidi, and Rolland Baker. *Always Enough: God's Miraculous Provision Among the Poorest Children on Earth.* Grand Rapids, MI: Chosen Books, 2002.

———. *The Hungry Always Get Fed: A Year of Miracles.* Chichester, UK: New Vine Press, 2007.

Bales, Kevin. *Disposable People: New Slavery in the Global Economy.* Berkeley, CA: University of California Press, 1999.

Barrs, Jerram. *The Heart of Evangelism.* Wheaton, IL: Crossway Books, 2001.

Bass, Diana Butler. *Christianity After Religion: The End of Church and the Birth of a New Spiritual Awakening.* New York: HarperCollins Publishers, 2012.

———. *A People's History of Christianity: The Other Side of the Story.* New York: HarperCollins Publishers, 2009.

Beaver, R. Pierce. *All Loves Excelling.* Grand Rapids, MI: Wm. B. Eerdmans, 1968.

———. Foreword to *Lamps Are For Lighting: The Story of Helen Barrett Montgomery and Lucy Waterbury Peabody* by Louise A. Cattan. Grand Rapids, MI: Wm. B. Eerdmans, 1972.

Bennis, Warren G., and Robert J. Thomas. *Geeks and Geezers: How Era, Values and Defining Moments Shape Leaders.* Boston, MA: Harvard Business School Press, 2002.

Benson, Robert. *In Constant Prayer.* Nashville, TN: Thomas Nelson, 2008.

Berger, Rose Marie. "What the Heck is Social Justice?" *Sojourners* 36 no. 2 (February 2007) 11.

———. *Who Killed Donte Manning? The Story of an American Neighborhood.* Baltimore, MD: Apprentice House, 2010.

Berrigan, Daniel. *Exodus: Let My People Go.* Eugene, OR: Cascade Books, 2008.

———. *They Call Us Dead Men: Reflections on Life and Conscience*. New York: Macmillan, 1966.

Berrigan, Philip. *Widen the Prison Gates: Writing from Jails April 1970–December 1972*. New York: Simon and Schuster, 1973.

Berrigan, Philip, and Elizabeth McAlister. *The Time's Discipline: The Beatitudes and Nuclear Resistance*. Eugene, OR: Wipf and Stock Publishers, 1989.

Bessenecker, Scott A. *The New Friars: The Emerging Movement Serving the World's Poor*. Downers Grove, IL: InterVarsity Press, 2006.

Bevans, Stephen B. *Models of Contextual Theology, Faith and Cultures*. Maryknoll, NY: Orbis Books. 2006.

Bevans, Stephen B., and Roger P. Schroeder. *Prophetic Dialogue: Reflections on Christian Mission Today*. Maryknoll, NY: Orbis Books, 2011.

Bolman, Lee G., and Terrence E. Deal. *Reframing Organizations: Artistry, Choice and Leadership*. 3rd ed. San Francisco, CA: Jossey-Bass Publishing, 2003.

Bono. *On the Move*. Nashville, TN: W Publishing Group, 2006.

Booth, Evangeline. *Love Is All*. New York: Press of Reliance Trading Company, 1908.

Bosch, Annemie. "Suffering for Justice: How Can We Anticipate and Pay the Price of Seeking Justice?" In *The Justice Project*, edited by Brian McLaren, Elisa Padilla, and Ashley Bunting Seeber, 216–23. Grand Rapids, MI: Baker Books, 2009.

Bosch, David J. *Believing in the Future: Toward a Missiology of Western Culture*. Valley Forge, PA: Trinity Press International, 1995.

———. *A Spirituality of the Road*. Scottsdale, PA: Herald Press, 1979.

———. *Transforming Mission: Paradigm Shifts in Theology of Mission*. Maryknoll, NY: Orbis Books, 1991.

———. *Witness to the World: The Christian Mission in Theological Perspective*. Eugene, OR: Wipf and Stock Publishers, 1980.

Bowie, Fiona, Deborah Kirkwood, and Shirley Ardener, eds. *Women and Missions: Past and Present, Anthropological and Historical Perceptions*. Oxford, UK: Berg Publishers, 1993.

Boyd, Andrew. *Baroness Cox: A Voice for the Voiceless*. Oxford, England: Lion Hudson Books, 1998.

Boyd-MacMillan, Ronald. *Faith That Endures: The Essential Guide to the Persecuted Church*. Grand Rapids, MI: Revell Books, 2006.

Brafman, Ori, and Rod A. Beckstrom. *The Starfish and the Spider: The Unstoppable Power of Leaderless Organizations*. London: Penguin Books, 2006.

Brewin, Kester. *Signs of Emergence: A Vision for Church that is Organic/Networked/Bottom-Up/Communal/Flexible and Always Evolving*. Grand Rapids, MI: Baker Books, 2007.

Brewington, Carla. "Two Communities." Unpublished manuscript, 1976 (hard copy, paper file).

Briggs, Jimmie. *Innocents Lost: When Child Soldiers Go to War*. New York: Basic Books, 2005.

Brodsky, Anne E. *With All Our Strength: The Revolutionary Association of the Women of Afghanistan*. New York: Routledge, 2002.

Broomhall, Marshall. *Last Letters and Further Records of Martyred Missionaries of the China Inland Mission*. London: Morgan and Scott, 1901.

Brueggemann, Walter. *Cadences of Home: Preaching among Exiles*. Louisville, KY: Westminster John Knox Press, 1997.

———. *Hopeful Imagination: Prophetic Voices in Exile*. Philadelphia, PA: Fortress Press, 1986.

———. "Preaching to Exiles." In *Exilic Preaching: Testimony for Christian Exiles in an Increasingly Hostile Culture*, edited by Erskine Clarke, 9–28. Harrisburg, PA: Trinity Press International, 2010.

———. *The Prophetic Imagination*. Philadelphia, PA: Fortress Press, 1978.

———. *Remember You Are Dust*. Eugene, OR: Cascade Books, 2012.

———. *Truth-Telling as Subversive Obedience*. Eugene, OR: Cascade Books, 2011.

Bunch, Charlotte. *Passionate Politics: 1968–1986*. New York: St. Martin's Press, 1987.

Bunch, Charlotte, and Niamh Reilly. *Demanding Accountability: The Global Campaign and Vienna Tribunal for Women's Human Rights*. New Brunswick, NJ: Center for Women's Global Leadership, Rutgers University, 1994.

Burger, Delores T. *Women Who Changed the Heart of the City*. Grand Rapids, MI: Kregel Publications, 1997.

Burgess, Alan. *The Small Woman*. London: Evans Brothers, 1957.

Cable, Mildred, and Francesca French. *The Red Lama*. London: China Inland Mission, 1933.

———. *Something Happened*. London: Hodder and Stoughton, 1933.

———. *Towards Spiritual Maturity: A Book For Those Who Seek It*. London: Hodder and Stoughton, 1939.

Cable, Mildred, Evangeline French, and Francesca French. *A Desert Journal: Letters From Central Asia*. London: Constable and Co., 1934.

Campbell, Greg. *Blood Diamonds: Tracing the Deadly Path of the World's Most Precious Stones*. Cambridge, MA: Basic Books, 2004.

Campbell, Will D., and Richard C. Goods. *Crashing the Idols*. Eugene, OR: Cascade Books, 2010.

Carey, William. *Adventures in Tibet: Including the Diary of Miss Annie R. Taylor's Remarkable Journey*. Toronto: William Briggs, 1902.

Carmichael, Amy. *Gold Cord: The Story of a Fellowship*. London: SPCK, 1932.

Cattan, Louise A. *Lamps Are For Lighting: The Story of Helen Barrett Montgomery and Lucy Waterbury Peabody*. Grand Rapids, MI: Wm. B. Eerdmans, 1972.

Cheadle, Don, and John Prendergast. *Not On Our Watch: The Mission to End Genocide in Darfur and Beyond*. New York: Hyperion, 2007.

Chevreau, Guy. *Turnings: The Kingdom of God and the Western World*. Tonbridge, England: Sovereign World, 2004.

Chittister, Joan. *The Liturgical Year: The Spiraling Adventure of the Spiritual Life*. Nashville, TN: Thomas Nelson, 2009.

Christman, Henry M., ed. *This Is Our Strength: The Selected Papers of Golda Meir*. New York: Macmillan, 1962.

Chryssaygis, John. *In The Heart of The Desert: The Spirituality of the Desert Fathers and Mothers*. Bloomington, IN: World Wisdom, 2003.

Clark, Elizabeth A. *Women in the Early Church*. Collegeville, MN: Liturgical Press, 1983.

Clarke, Erskine, ed. *Exilic Preaching: Testimony for Christian Exiles in an Increasingly Hostile Culture*. Harrisburg, PA: Trinity Press International, 1998.

Codrington, F. I. *Hot-Hearted*. London: Church of England, Zenana Missionary Society, no date.

Collins, Larry, and Dominique Lapierre. *O Jerusalem*. New York: Simon and Schuster, 1972.

Comblin, Jose. *Cry of the Oppressed, Cry of Jesus: Meditations on Scripture and Contemporary Struggle*. Maryknoll, NY: Orbis Books, 1988.

———. *The Holy Spirit and Liberation*. Eugene, OR: Wipf and Stock Publishers, 1989.

———. *The Meaning of Mission: Jesus, Christians and the Wayfaring Church*. Maryknoll, NY: Orbis Books, 1977.

———. *Sent From the Father: Meditations on the Fourth Gospel*. Maryknoll, NY: Orbis Books, 1974.

Costas, Orlando E. *Christ Outside the Gate: Mission Beyond Christendom*. Maryknoll, NY: Orbis Books, 1992.

———. *Liberating News: A Theology of Contextual Evangelization*. Eugene, OR: Wipf and Stock Publishers, 1989.

Cox, Baroness Caroline, and Dr. John Marks. *This Immoral Trade: Slavery in the 21st Century*. Oxford, UK: Monarch Books, 2006.

Creegan, Nicola Hoggard, and Christine D. Pohl. *Living on the Boundaries: Evangelical Women, Feminism and the Theological Academy*. Downers Grove, IL: InterVarsity Press, 2005.

Cullinan, Colleen Carpenter. *Redeeming the Story: Women, Suffering and Christ*. New York: Continuum International, 2004.

Dante Alighieri. c.1313–1321. *The Divine Comedy*. Vol. 3. *Paradiso*. Charles E. Norton, trans. Boston, MA: Houghton Mifflin (1898). Online: http://www.archive.org/stream/divinecomedyofda03dantiala#page/n5/mode/2up. Accessed April 6, 2011.

Davey, Cyril. *Never Say Die: The Story of Gladys Aylward*. London: Christian Literature Crusade, 1964.

Dawson, Canon. *Missionary Heroines of the Cross*. London: Seeley, Service and Co., 1930.

Day, Dorothy. *The Long Loneliness*. New York: Harper and Row, 1952.

Dorr, Donal. *Faith at Work: A Spirituality of Leadership*. Dublin, Ireland: Columba Press, 2006.

Dr. Agnes Henderson of Nagpur: A Story of Medical Pioneer Work. Glasgow, Scotland: United Free Church of Scotland, Women's Foreign Mission Publications, 1927.

Earle, Mary C. *The Desert Mothers: Spiritual Practices from the Women of the Wilderness*. New York: Morehouse Publishing, 2007.

Ellis, Marc H. *Practicing Exile: The Religious Odyssey of an American Jew*. Minneapolis, MN: Fortress Press, 2002.

Escobar, Samuel. *The New Global Mission: The Gospel from Everywhere to Everyone*. Downers Grove, IL: InterVarsity Press, 2003.

Evans, Sara M., ed. *Journeys That Opened Up the World: Women, Student Christian Movements and Social Justice*. Rutgers, NJ: Rutgers University Press, 2003.

Forman, Mary. *Praying with the Desert Mothers*. Collegeville, MN: Liturgical Press, 2005.

Frost, Michael. *Exiles: Living Missionally in a Post-Modern Culture*. Peabody, MA: Hendrickson Publishers, 2006.

Gadamer, Hans-Georg. *Philosophical Hermeneutics*. Berkeley, CA: University of California Press, 1976.

Gallagher, Robert L., and Paul Hertig, eds. *Mission in Acts: Ancient Narratives in Contemporary Context*. Maryknoll, NY: Orbis Books, 2004.

Garrison, Becky. *Jesus Died for This? A Satirist Search for the Risen Christ*. Grand Rapids, MI: Zondervan, 2010.

Gerlach, Luther P., and Virginia H. Hine. *People, Power, Change Movements of Social Transformation*. Indianapolis, IN: Bobbs-Merrill Company, 1970.

Glasser, Arthur. *Announcing the Kingdom: The Story of God's Mission in the Bible.* Grand Rapids, MI: Baker Academic, 2003.

Glover, Robert H. *The Progress of World-Wide Missions.* New York: George H. Doran Company, 1924.

Gold, Dore. *The Fight for Jerusalem.* Washington, DC: Regnery Publishing, 2007.

Goll, Michal Ann. *Women on the Front Lines.* Shippensburg, PA: Destiny Image Publishers, 1999.

Gracey, J. T. *Eminent Missionary Women.* New York: Eaton and Mains, 1898.

Gregory of Nazianzus, "Letter 4 to Basil." In The Fathers Speak: St. Basil the Great, St. Gregory of Nazianzus, St. Gregory of Nyssa, edited by George A. Barrois, 18–19. Crestwood, NY: St. Vladimir's Seminary Press, 1986.

Grondin, Jean. *Hans-Georg Gadamer: A Biography.* Translated by Joel Weinsheimer. Yale Studies in Hermeneutics. New Haven, CT: Yale University Press, 2003.

Gupta, Paul R., and Sherwood G. Lingenfelter. *Breaking Tradition to Accomplish Mission: Training Leaders for A Church-Planting Movement.* Winona Lake, IN: BMH Books, 2006.

Gutierrez, Gustavo. *A Theology of Liberation: History, Politics and Salvation.* Maryknoll, NY: Orbis Books, 1988.

Hall, Douglas John. *The Cross in Our Context: Jesus and the Suffering World.* Minneapolis, MN: Fortress Press, 2003.

Hanlon, Gail, ed. *Voicing Power: Conversations with Visionary Women.* Oxford, UK: Westview Press, 1997.

Harmless, William. *Desert Christians: An Introduction to the Literature of Early Monasticism.* New York: Oxford University Press, 2004.

Harper, Ida Husted. *The Life and Work of Susan B. Anthony.* Indianapolis, IN: Hollenbeck Press, 1898.

Hauerwas, Stanley, and William H. Willimon. *Resident Aliens: A Provocative Assessment of Culture and Ministry for People Who Know That Something Is Wrong.* Nashville, TN: Abingdon Press, 1989.

Haugen, Gary. *Just Courage: God's Great Expedition for the Restless Christian.* Downers Grove, IL: IVP Books, 2008.

Hayes, John B. *Submerge: Living Deep in a Shallow World.* Ventura, CA: Regal Books, 2006.

Hazelton, Lesley. "Doris Lessing on Feminism, Communism and 'Space Fiction.'" Review of Canopus in Argos: Archives, by Doris Lessing. *New York Times,* July 25, 1982, http://www.nytimes.com/books/99/01/10/specials/lessing-space.html.

Heath, Elaine. *The Mystic Way of Evangelism: A Contemplative Vision for Christian Outreach.* Grand Rapids, MI: Baker Academic, 2008.

Helgesen, Sally. *The Web of Inclusion: Architecture for Building Great Organizations.* Washington, DC: Beard Books, 1995.

Hendricks, Obery M., Jr. *The Politics of Jesus.* New York: Doubleday, 2006.

Heppner, Kevin, and Jo Becker. *"My Gun Was As Tall As Me": Child Soldiers in Burma.* New York: Human Rights Watch, 2002.

Heschel, Abraham Joshua. *The Prophets.* New York: Harper and Row, 1962.

Hewitt, Lyndi, and Holly J. McCammon. "Explaining Suffrage Mobilization: Balance, Neutralization, and Range in Collective Action Frames." In *Frames of Protest: Social Movements and the Framing Perspective,* edited by Hank Johnston and John A. Noakes, 33–52. Lanham, MD: Rowan and Littlefield, 2005.

Hiebert, Paul G. *Missiological Implications of Epistemological Shifts.* Harrisburg, PA: Trinity Press International, 1999.

Hirsch, Alan. *The Forgotten Ways.* Grand Rapids, MI: Brazos Press, 2006.

Houghton, Frank L. *Amy Carmichael of Dohnavur.* London: SPCK, 1954.

Houston, James, M. *Joyful Exiles: Life in Christ on the Dangerous Edge of Things.* Downers Grove, IL: IVP Books, 2006.

Huber, Mary Taylor, and Nancy C. Lutkehaus, eds. *Gendered Missions: Women and Men in Missionary Discourse and Practice.* Ann Arbor, MI: University of Michigan Press, 1999.

Hudson, Jocee. "Parashat Sh'mot—Spiritual Exile." January 10, 2010. No pages. Online: http://rabbihudson.blogspot.com/2010/01/parashat-shmot-spiritual-exile.html.

Hull, Alison, ed. *Thinking Aloud: Keswick Lectures.* Cumbria, UK: Authentic Lifestyle, 2002.

The Inn of the Sixth Happiness. Film. Directed by Mark Robson, produced by Buddy Adler, starring Ingrid Bergman, Robert Donat, and Curd Jürgens. Century City, CA: Twentieth Century Fox, 1958.

Jackson, John. *Mary Reed, Missionary to the Lepers.* London: Mission to the Lepers, 1899.

Joh, Wanhee Anne. *Heart of the Cross: A Postcolonial Christology.* Louisville, KY: Westminster John Knox Press, 2006.

Johnston, Hank, and John A. Noakes, eds. *Frames of Protest: Social Movements and the Framing Perspective.* Lanham, MD: Rowan and Littlefield, 2005.

Keel, Tim. *Intuitive Leadership: Embracing a Paradigm of Narrative, Metaphor and Chaos.* Grand Rapids, MI: Baker Books, 2007.

Keller, Timothy. *The Prodigal God: Recovering the Heart of the Christian Faith.* New York: Dutton, 2008.

Kellerman, Barbara. *Followership: How Followers are Creating Change and Changing Leaders.* Boston, MA: Harvard Business School Press, 2008.

Kellerman, Bill Wylie, ed. *A Keeper of the Word: Selected Writings of William Stringfellow.* Grand Rapids, MI: Wm. B. Eerdmans, 1994.

Kelley, Joseph T. *Faith in Exile: Seeking Hope in Times of Doubt.* Mahwah, NJ: Paulist Press, 2003.

Knight, F. M. *The Shout of a King: A True Story of the Zenana Bible and Medical Mission.* London: Hodder and Stoughton, 1938.

Koehler, Karen. "Angels of History Carrying Bricks: Gropius in Exile." In *The Dispossessed: An Anatomy of Exile,* edited by Peter I. Rose, 257–80. Boston, MA: University of Massachusetts Press, 2005.

Kraemer, Ross Shepard, and Mary Rose D'Angelo, eds. *Women and Christian Origins.* Oxford, UK: Oxford University Press, 1999.

Labberton, Mark. *The Dangerous Act of Loving Your Neighbor.* Downers Grove, IL: InterVarsity Press, 2010.

———. *The Dangerous Act of Worship: Living God's Call to Justice.* Downers Grove, IL: InterVarsity Press, 2007.

Lambert, John C. *Missionary Heroes in Asia.* Philadelphia, PA: J. B. Lippincott Company, 1908.

Lane, Belden C. *The Solace of Fierce Landscapes: Exploring Desert and Mountain Spirituality.* Oxford, England: Oxford University Press, 1998.

Latham, R. O. *Gladys Aylward: One of the Undefeated.* London: Edinburgh House Press, 1950.

Laughery, Gregory J. *Living Hermeneutics in Motion: An Analysis and Evaluation of Paul Ricoeur's Contribution to Biblical Hermeneutics.* Lanham, MD: University Press of America, 2002.

Leech, Kenneth. *We Preach Christ Crucified.* New York: Church Publishing, 1994.

Lingenfelter, Sherwood G. *Leading Cross-Culturally: Covenant Relationships for Effective Christian Leadership.* Grand Rapids, MI: Baker Academic, 2008.

The Lives of the Spiritual Mothers. Buena Vista, CO: Holy Apostles Convent, 1991.

Logan, Harriet. *Unveiled: Voices of Women in Afghanistan.* New York: HarperCollins Publishers, 2002.

MacLeod, Judith. *Women's Union Missionary Society: The Story of a Continuing Mission.* Upper Darby, PA: InterServe International Fellowship, 1999.

Malone, Mary T. *Women and Christianity: The First Thousand Years.* Vol. 1. Maryknoll, NY: Orbis Books, 2000.

Marsh, Charles. *The Beloved Community: How Faith Shapes Social Justice, from the Civil Rights Movement to Today.* New York: Perseus Books, 2005.

McAlister, Elizabeth. "Preach the Good News and Cast Out Demons: On Civil Resistance." No pages. Online: http://www.thewitness.org/agw/mcalister022704.html.

McDonnell, Faith J. H., and Grace Akallo. *Girl Soldier: A Story of Hope for Northern Uganda's Children.* Grand Rapids, MI: Chosen Books, 2007.

McGill, Arthur C. *Suffering: A Test of Theological Method.* Eugene, OR: Wipf and Stock Publishers, 1982.

McKnight, Scot. *Fasting.* Nashville, TN: Thomas Nelson, 2009.

McLaren, Brian. *Finding Our Way Again: The Return of the Ancient Practices.* Nashville, TN: Thomas Nelson, 2008.

McLaren, Brian, Elisa Padilla, and Ashley Bunting Seeber. *The Justice Project.* Grand Rapids, MI: Baker Books, 2009.

McNeill Donald P., Douglas A. Morrison, and Henri J. M. Nouwen. *Compassion: A Reflection on the Christian Life.* Garden City, NY: Image Books, 1983.

Mehta, Sunita. *Women for Afghan Women.* New York: Palgrave Macmillan, 2002.

Meir, Golda. *A Land of Our Own.* Philadelphia, PA: Jewish Publication Society of America, 1973.

Meroff, Deborah. *True Grit: Women Taking on the World, for God's Sake.* Milton Keynes, UK: Authentic Media, 2004.

Milavec, Aaron. *The Didache: Faith, Hope and Life of the Earliest Christian Communities, 50–70 C.E.* New York: Newman Press, 2003.

Miller, Luree. *On Top of the World: Five Women Explorers in Tibet.* Seattle, WA: Mountaineers, 1984.

Montgomery, Helen Barrett. *The Bible and Missions.* Cambridge, MA: Central Committee on the United Study of Foreign Missions, 1920.

———. *From Jerusalem to Jerusalem.* Cambridge, MA: Central Committee on the United Study of Foreign Missions, 1929.

———. *The King's Highway: A Study of Present Conditions on the Foreign Field.* West Medford, MA: Central Committee on the United Study of Foreign Missions, 1915.

———. *Prayer and Missions.* West Medford, MA: Central Committee on the United Study of Foreign Missions, 1924.

———. *Western Women in Eastern Lands.* New York: Macmillan, 1910.

Morris, Aldon D., and Carol McClung Mueller, eds. *Frontiers in Social Movement Theory.* New Haven, CT: Yale University Press, 1992.

Mother Teresa and Brian Kolodiejchuk. *Mother Teresa: Come Be My Light—The Private Writings of the "Saint of Calcutta."* New York: Doubleday, 2007.

Mursell, Gordon. *Praying in Exile.* London: Darton, Longman, and Todd, 2005.

Newbigin, Lesslie. "Can The West Be Converted?" International Bulletin of Missionary Research (January). New Haven, CT: Overseas Ministries Study Center, 1987.

———. *The Open Secret: An Introduction to the Theology of Mission.* Grand Rapids, MI: Wm. B. Eerdmans, 1978.

———. *Truth to Tell: The Gospel as Public Truth.* Grand Rapids, MI: Wm. B. Eerdmans, 1991.

Nissen, Johannes. *New Testament and Mission: Historical and Hermeneutical Perspectives.* Frankfurt, Germany: Peter Lang, 1999.

Norris, Richard A., Jr., ed. *The Song of Songs: Interpreted by Early Christian and Medieval Commentators.* Grand Rapids, MI: Wm B. Eerdmans, 2003.

O'Conner, Kathleen M. *Lamentations and the Tears of the World.* Maryknoll, NY: Orbis Books, 2006.

O'Kane, Mary. "Borderlands and Women: Transversal Political Agency on the Burma-Thailand Border." Working Paper no. 126. Center for Southeast Asian Studies. Victoria, Australia: Monash University Press, 2005.

Oldham, J. H. *Florence Allshorn and the Story of St. Julian's.* London: SCM Press, 1951.

Pannell, William. *My Friend the Enemy.* Waco, TX: Word Press, 1968.

Parkman, Mary R. *Heroines of Service.* New York: Century Co., 1918.

Penn-Lewis, Jesse. *The Story of Job.* Bournemouth, England: Overcomer Book Room, 1903.

Perkins, Dennis N. T. *Leading at the Edge: Leadership Lessons from the Extraordinary Saga of Shackleton's Antarctic Expedition.* New York: American Management Association, 2000.

Phillips, James, and Robert Coote, eds. "Reflection on Biblical Models of Mission." In *Toward the Twenty-first Century in Christian Mission*, edited by James Phillips and Robert Coote, 175–76. Grand Rapids, MI: Wm. B. Eerdmans, 1993.

Pickard, Stephen K. *Liberating Evangelism: Gospel Theology and the Dynamics of Communication.* Harrisburg, PA: Trinity Press International, 1999.

Pierson, Arthur T. *The Modern Mission Century.* New York: Baker and Taylor Company, 1901.

Pierson, Paul Everett. *The Dynamics of Christian Mission: History Through a Missiological Perspective.* Pasadena, CA: William Carey International University Press, 2009.

Pollock, J. C. *Shadows Fall Apart: The Story of the Zenana Bible and Medical Mission.* London: Hodder and Stoughton, 1958.

Polner, Murray, and Jim O'Grady. *Disarmed and Dangerous: The Radical Lives and Times of Daniel and Philip Berrigan.* New York: Basic Books, 1997.

Poplin, Mary. *Finding Calcutta.* Downers Grove, IL: Veritas Forum Books, 1988.

Potts, Margaret, and St. Julian's Community, eds. *The Notebooks of Florence Allshorn.* London: SCM Press, 1957.

Pullinger, Jackie. *Crack in the Wall.* London: Hodder and Stoughton, 1989.

Pullinger, Jackie, and Andrew Quicke. *Chasing the Dragon.* London: Hodder and Stoughton, 1980.

Ranft, Patricia. *Women and Spiritual Equality in Christian Tradition.* New York: St. Martin's Press, 1998.

Rhodes, Jacqueline. *Radical Feminism, Writing and Critical Agency: Manifesto to Modem*. Albany, NY: State University of New York Press, 2005.

Rijnhart, Susie C. *With the Tibetans in Tent and Temple*. London: Oliphant, Anderson and Ferrier, 1902.

Robert, Dana L. *American Women in Mission: A Social History of Their Thought and Practice*. Macon, GA: Mercer University Press, 1997.

———. *Christian Mission: How Christianity Became a World Mission*. Chichester, UK: Wiley-Blackwell, 2009.

———. *Gospel Bearers, Gender Barriers: Missionary Women in the Twentieth Century*. Maryknoll, NY: Orbis Books, 2002.

———. "Revisioning the Women's Missionary Movement." In *The Good News of the Kingdom: Mission Theology for the Third Millennium*, edited by Charles E. Van Engen, Dean S. Gilliland, and Paul E. Pierson, 109–18. Eugene, OR: Wipf and Stock Publishers, 1999.

Robson, Isabel S. *Two Lady Missionaries in Tibet*. London, UK: S. W. Partridge and Company, 1911.

Rosen, David M. *Armies of the Young: Child Soldiers in War and Terrorism*. New Brunswick, NJ: Rutgers University Press, 2005.

Roxburgh, Alan J. *Missional Map-Making: Skills for Leading in Times of Tradition*. San Francisco, CA: Jossey-Bass Publishing, 2010.

———. *The Sky Is Falling: Leaders Lost in Transition*. Eagle, ID: ACI Publishing.

Said, Edward W. *Reflections on Exile and Other Essays*. Cambridge, MA: Harvard University Press, 2000.

Schwartz, Michael, and Shuva Paul. "Resource Mobilization Versus the Mobilization of People: Why Consensus Movements Cannot Be Instruments of Social Change." In *Frontiers in Social Movement Theory*, edited by Aldon D. Morris and Carol McClung Mueller, 205–23. New Haven, CT: Yale University Press, 1992.

Shaw, Luci. *The Crime of Living Cautiously: Hearing God's Call to Adventure*. Downers Grove, IL: InterVarsity Press, 2005.

Shenk, Wilbert R. *Changing Frontiers of Mission*. Maryknoll, NY: Orbis Books, 1998.

———. "Paying Attention to People as Gratitude." In *The Three Tasks of Leadership: Worldly Wisdom for Pastoral Leaders*, edited by Eric O. Jacobsen, 171–79. Grand Rapids, MI: Wm. B. Eerdmans, 2009.

———. *Write the Vision: The Church Renewed*. Eugene, OR: Wipf and Stock Publishers, 2001.

Shenk, Wilbert R. ed. *Enlarging the Story: Perspectives on Writing World Christian History*. Maryknoll, NY: Orbis Books, 2002.

———. *The Transfiguration of Mission*. Scottsdale, PA: Herald Press, 1993.

———. *Write the Vision: The Church Renewed*. Eugene, OR: Wipf and Stock Publishers, 1995.

Shuster, Marguerite. "Leadership as Interpreting Reality." In *The Three Tasks of Leadership: Worldly Wisdom for Pastoral Leaders*, edited by Eric O. Jacobsen, 17–23. Grand Rapids, MI: Wm. B. Eerdmans, 2009.

Sider, Ronald J. *The Scandal of the Evangelical Conscience: Why Are Christians Living Just Like the Rest of the World*. Grand Rapids, MI: Baker Books, 2005.

Simpson, John, ed. *The Oxford Book of Exile*. Oxford, England: Oxford University Press, 1995.

Singer, P. W. *Children at War*. Berkeley, CA: University of California Press, 2006.

Skidmore, Monique, and Patricia Lawrence, eds. *Women and the Contested State: Religion, Violence and Agency in South and Southeast Asia*. Notre Dame, IN: University of Notre Dame Press, 2007.

Skillen, James W. *A Covenant to Keep: Meditations on the Biblical Theme of Justice*. Grand Rapids, MI: CRC Publications, 1998.

Smith-Christopher, Daniel L. *A Biblical Theology of Exile*. Minneapolis, MN: Fortress Press, 2002.

Snow, David A., and Robert D. Benford. "Ideology, Frame Resonance, and Participant Mobilization." In *International Social Movement Research: From Structure to Action*, edited by Bert Klandermans, Hanspeter Kreisi, and Sidney Tarrow, 197–212. Greenwich, CT: JAI Press, 1988.

Spina, Frank Anthony. *The Faith of the Outsider: Exclusion and Inclusion in the Biblical Story*. Grand Rapids, MI: Wm. B. Eerdmans, 2005.

Stengel, Richard. "Mandela: His Eight lessons of Leadership." *Time* 172 no. 1 (Sept. 2008) 43–48.

Stott, John. *Christian Mission in the Modern World*. Downers Grove: IL: InterVarsity Press, 1975.

Stringfellow, William. *Free in Obedience: The Radical Christian Life*. New York: Seabury Press, 1964.

Swan, Laura. *The Forgotten Desert Mothers*. New York: Paulist Press, 2001.

Sweetman, Caroline, ed. *Women and Leadership*. Oxford, UK: Oxfam Publication, 2000.

Taylor, Annie R. "The Degradation of the Women." In *China's Millions* (1887).

———. *Pioneering in Tibet: The Origin and Progress of "The Tibetan Pioneer Mission" together with My Experiences in Tibet, and Some Facts about The Country*. London: Morgan and Scott, 1895.

Taylor, Barbara Brown. *Leaving Church: A Memoir of Faith*. San Francisco, CA: HarperCollins, 2006.

Thiselton, Anthony C. *Hermeneutics: An Introduction*. Grand Rapids, MI: Wm. B. Eerdmans, 2009.

Thomas, Robert J. *Crucibles of Leadership: How to Learn from Experience to Become a Great Leader*. Boston, MA: Harvard Business Press, 2008.

Thompson, Phyllis. *Desert Pilgrim: Mildred Cable's Venture for God in Central Asia*. London: China Inland Mission, 1957.

———. *A London Sparrow: The Story of Gladys Aylward*. London: Word Books, 1971.

Tiersma-Watson, Jude. "Mother Teresa: To Suffer with Joy." In *Footprints of God: A Narrative Theology of Mission*, edited by Charles Van Engen, Nancy Thomas, and Robert Gallagher, 114–23. Monrovia, CA: MARC, 1999.

Tilly, Charles. *From Mobilization to Revolution*. New York: McGraw-Hill, 1978.

Tilly, Charles, and Lesley J. Wood. *Social Movements: 1768–2008*. Boulder, CO: Paradigm Publishers, 2009.

Tiltman, Marjorie Hessell. *God's Adventurers*. London: George G. Harrap and Co., 1933.

Tomlin, Graham. Foreword to *Prepare for Exile: A New Spirituality for the Church*, by Patrick Whitworth, xii. London: SPCK, 2008.

Trebesch, Shelley. *Isolation: A Place of Transformation in the Life of a Leader*. Altadena, CA: Barnabas Publishers, 1997.

Trueblood, Elton. *The Yoke of Christ and Other Sermons*. New York: Harper and Brothers, 1958.

Tuck, J. Erskine, ed. *This is My Story*. London: Henry E. Walter, 1955.

Tucker, Ruth A. *Daughters of the Church: Women and Ministry from New Testament Times to the Present*. Grand, Rapids, MI: Zondervan, 1987.

———. *From Jerusalem to Irian Jaya: A Biographical History of Christian Missions*. Grand, Rapids, MI: Zondervan, 1987.

———. *Guardians of the Great Commission: The Story of Women in Modern Missions*. Grand Rapids, MI: Zondervan, 1988.

———. *Leadership Reconsidered: Becoming a Person of Influence*. Grand Rapids, MI: Baker Books, 2008.

———. *Women in the Maze: Questions and Answers on Biblical Equality*. Downers Grove, IL: InterVarsity Press, 1992.

Tutu, Desmond. *No Future Without Forgiveness*. New York: Doubleday, 1999.

Van Engen, Charles. *God's Missionary People: Rethinking the Purpose of the Local Church*. Grand Rapids, MI: Baker Books, 1991.

———. *Mission On The Way*. Grand Rapids, MI: Baker Books, 2000.

Van Engen, Charles, Nancy Thomas, and Robert Gallagher, eds. *Footprints of God: A Narrative Theology of Mission*. Monrovia, CA: MARC, 1999.

Vanier, Jean. *Befriending the Stranger*. Grand Rapids, MI: Wm. B. Eerdmans, 2001.

Volf, Miroslav. *The End of Memory: Remembering Rightly in a Violent World*. Grand Rapids, MI: Wm. B. Eerdmans, 2006.

———. *Exclusion and Embrace: A Theological Exploration of Identity, Otherness and Reconciliation*. Nashville, TN: Abingdon Press, 1996.

———. *Free of Charge: Giving and Forgiving in a Culture Stripped of Grace*. Grand Rapids, MI: Zondervan, 2005.

———. *The Future of Hope: Christian Tradition amid Modernity and Postmodernity*. Grand Rapids, MI: Wm. B. Eerdmans, 2004.

Wallis, Jim. *Agenda for Biblical People*. San Francisco, CA: Harper and Row, 1976.

———. *The Call to Conversion: Recovering the Gospel for These Times*. New York: Harper and Row, 1981.

———. *Faith Works: Lessons from the Life of an Activist Preacher*. New York: Random House, 2000.

———. *God's Politics: Why the Right Gets it Wrong and the Left Doesn't Get It*. New York: HarperCollins Publishers, 2005.

———. *The Soul of Politics*. Maryknoll, NY: Orbis Books, 1994.

———. *Who Speaks for God?* New York: Delacorte Press, 1996.

Wallis, Jim, and Joyce Hollyday, eds. *Cloud of Witnesses*. Maryknoll NY: Orbis Books, 1991.

Walls, Andrew F. *The Cross-Cultural Process in Christian History*. Maryknoll, NY: Orbis Books, 2002.

———. *The Missionary Movement in Christian History*. Maryknoll, NY: Orbis Books, 1996.

Watters, David E. *At The Foot of the Snows*. Poulsbo, WA: Engage Faith Press, 2011.

Ward, Benedicta. *Harlots of the Desert: A Study of Repentance in Early Monastic Sources*. Kalamazoo, MI: Cistercian Publications, 1987.

Weaver, Alain Epp. *States of Exile: Visions of Diaspora, Witness and Return*. Scottsdale, PA: Herald Press, 2008.

Wessells, Michael. *Child Soldiers: From Violence to Protection*. Cambridge, MA: Harvard University Press, 2006.

West, Cornel. *Democracy Matters*. New York: Penguin Books, 2004.

Bibliography

Westphal, Merold. *Whose Community? Which Interpretation? Philosophical Hermeneutics for the Church.* Grand Rapids, MI: Baker Academic, 2009.

Whitworth, Patrick. *Prepare for Exile: A New Spirituality for the Church.* London: SPCK, 2008.

Wiesel, Elie. *Messengers of God: Biblical Portraits and Legends.* New York: Random House, 1976.

———. *Night.* New York: Farrar, Straus and Giroux, 1958.

Wilson, Jesse R., ed. *Men and Women of Far Horizons.* New York: Friendship Press, 1935.

Winter, Nicholas J. G. *Dangerous Frames: How Ideas about Race and Gender Shape Public Opinion.* Chicago, IL: University of Chicago Press, 2008.

Woodberry, J. Dudley, ed. *Reaching the Resistant: Barriers and Bridges for Mission.* Evangelical Missionary Society Series, no. 6. Pasadena, CA: William Carey Library, 1998.

Wright, Christopher J. H. *The Mission of God: Unlocking the Bible's Grand Narrative.* Downers Grove, IL: IVP Academic, 2006.

Yoder, John Howard. *The Politics of Jesus.* Grand Rapids MI: Wm. B. Eerdmans, 1972.

Zwemer, Samuel M. *Evangelism Today: Message Not Method.* London: Fleming H. Revell, 1944.

———. *Islam and the Cross.* Phillipsburg, NJ: P and R Publishing, 2002.

———. *Taking Hold of God: Studies on the Nature, Need and Power of Prayer.* London: Marshall, Morgan, and Scott, 1936.

INDEX

Index

Printed in Great Britain
by Amazon

21613356R10098